Embracing the Love
God Wants You to Have

ALSO BY TAFFI DOLLAR

Authentic: Dare to Be Real

Your Spiritual Makeover

21 Days to Your Spiritual Makeover

*A Woman After God's Own Heart:
Fulfilling the Will of God for Your Life
and Empowering Those Around You*

The Portrait of a Virtuous Woman

Embracing the Love God Wants You to Have

A Life of Peace, Joy, and Victory

TAFFI DOLLAR

Amistad
An Imprint of HarperCollinsPublishers
www.harpercollins.com

HarperCollins books may be purchased for educational, business, or sales promotional use. For information, please e-mail the Special Markets Department at SPsales@harpercollins.com.

Excerpt from "Still I Rise" by Maya Angelou courtesy of Random House.

FIRST EDITION

Designed by Suet Yee Chong

Library of Congress Cataloging-in-Publication Data has been applied for.

ISBN: 978-0-06-231672-1

14 15 16 17 18 OV/RRD 10 9 8 7 6 5 4 3

Creflo, my hope and prayer is that you experience daily the fulfillment of our rock-solid bond. I thank my God above for sending you into my life and for our being able to share our lives together. It has been a reward and an undeniable joy knowing that we can face life's journeys together. It has been your heartfelt love and faith in me that has encouraged me to write this book. You've been a constant support of motivation and strength every day since I met you. I can never thank God enough for allowing our paths to cross almost thirty years ago. As my husband, Creflo, I want to thank you for showing me the unfailing love of God every single day. I am certainly a blessed woman because of you. You are an expression of God's love to me!

—*Taffi*

CONTENTS

INTRODUCTION

A FEW YEARS AGO, I BEGAN TO RECEIVE MANY profound revelations from God. While discussing revelations with my husband, Creflo, and studying the Word myself, I began to realize these insights from God were concerning grace. God revealed to me that His grace is a manifestation of love. Together, Creflo and I have applied this belief and as a result have experienced greater levels of joy and freedom than ever before. The revelation has been truly an amazing gift. Our deeper understanding of God's grace has helped us to understand each other better, and taught us how to listen to the Holy Spirit when resolving conflicts. We began to fully understand that there is a grace that allows us to flourish in all of our relationships. Grace allowed our love for each other to break barriers—of fear and misinformation—we learned in our families growing up. Grace allowed us to change the way we discipline, direct, and enjoy our children. Grace enabled us to go from trying to rule and control our children to discerning their God-given gifts and guiding them to fulfill their divine purposes in life.

There was a time when we argued about how much to give our children and how much to make them work for what they received. We both were taught, "If you want it, work for it." Our parents didn't—couldn't—give us a car to drive to high school. We had to walk or use public transportation. So it was difficult deciding when to give our children a car. I prayed long and hard about it, and God gave me peace with our decisions. Particularly in these days, when parents struggle against allowing our children to grow up feeling entitled to gifts and favors, I believe we can ask God to show us the right balance for each child, and that God will reveal what we should and should not give.

God's revelations on love and grace have been pouring forth in my life, and I thank God for the opportunities to share them. When we understand that we are loved by God, and that God gives us grace—favor beyond what we can earn—our relationships become transformed. When we feel loved, we glow. We smile more, we feel lighter, we eat less, we laugh louder. Imagine experiencing that "in love" feeling simply by meditating on God's love for you. When our heart feels content, we don't even eat as much junk food. There's nothing like the real thing. We're not eating to fill a void. When we are filled with God's love, we can extend more love in our relationships. I believe God's love and grace bless our relationships with our family and friends, and our relationships at church, at work, and in our communities.

Grace is a game changer. Grace is one of the things that can be experienced in our relationships, extended through our manners in dealing with people. I think it is time for all of us to see grace in our lives. We can show grace in the smile we give to a stranger on the street, a reminder that everyone in our world hasn't turned mean or mad. Grace is in a small bottle of scented lotion you leave on a coworker's desk to brighten her day. Grace is responding to someone else's anger with uncommon patience and pardon. Whether it's your child throwing a temper tantrum, or your boss firebreathing over your shoulder, when you have it down in your heart that God wants you to live in peace, you resolve to diffuse the anger that can react to it. Many of us have the misunderstanding that we can use fear and intimidation to control relationships. We think whoever yells the loudest wins. Not so.

In this book we will examine grace-based relationships versus fear-based relationships. I am learning that our relationships require love and grace to survive. Many marriages fail not because of a lack of love but because of an inability, or unwillingness, to adapt to changes and show the other grace. When situations come up that we can't manage, we need God's grace to get us through. The graceless relationships are the ones that end in destruction and despair.

Tina Turner sang, *"What's love got to do with it?"* Love's got everything to do with everything. We need healthy relationships to grow as human beings. Without loving relationships with family and friends we feel disconnected. Excessive isolation can lead to mental illness. In relating to other human beings, we express our thoughts and feelings and experience the thoughts and feelings of someone else. There's beauty in the exchange.

We need love and grace in our relationships. The Bible tells us, in 1 Corinthians 13:4–6, "Love is patient and kind; love does not envy or boast; it is not arrogant or rude. It does not insist on its own way; it is not irritable or resentful." In this book we will reflect on how we can expect, experience, and express God's love in the relationships in our lives. We will examine our love for God—and His love for us. We will reflect on self-love, and develop more loving relationships with our significant other, with our children, our family, our coworkers, neighbors, and fellow church members.

The Webster dictionary defines *grace* as, "divine favor toward man . . . divine love and pardon . . . the mercy of God, as distinguished from His justice." The Bible speaks often of God's grace. Hebrews 4:16 says, "Let us draw near to the throne of grace, that we may receive mercy and find grace to help in time of need."

In this book, you will see how God's grace shines in the

lives of other women, and you will be encouraged to reflect on your own experiences of God's grace.

When I received a deeper understanding of grace, I felt liberated. It took the pressure off of me and my own ability to have to measure up to what I believed His standards were. Even though I understood the role of the Holy Spirit, I felt a need to do things in my own strength. For example, I thought I had to do a lot of fasting and praying to cleanse myself before delivering a sermon. But when God gave me a revelation about grace, I realized I didn't need to put that sort of pressure on myself. Grace allows me to trust God's ability above my own. It all boils down to submitting ourselves to the Holy Spirit and allowing Him to be our guide. Within these chapters, I want to encourage you to begin to release the pressure you may be putting on yourself. I want you to begin to realize that there is a grace to help you fulfill all the roles you are destined to fulfill.

Experiencing God's love and grace in our life begins with changing the distorted way we view ourselves, and realizing we are uniquely created by God and we are valued by God. This book is specifically designed to help women receive personal revelation from God about love and grace in their relationships. You will be encouraged to have conversations with God, to speak to Him in your own language, but, more important, to listen to how God speaks to you. It is so vital to our relationships that we begin to take an honest look at ourselves and allow God's Holy Spirit to do a great work within us. When we allow God's love and grace in our life, we accept ourselves—flaws and all—without apology. We may also come to recognize that what we believe are flaws are part of the unique gifts that God has given.

Love and grace give us balance. With God's love and grace in our heart, our child's temporary lapse in judgment doesn't tip our whole universe off kilter; our husband's snide remark doesn't break our heart; our friends' need doesn't find us impatient, trying to rush them off the phone. When God's grace and love are fully present in our midst we feel better, we do better, and we find happiness.

I encourage you to get to know God for yourself. To open your heart and begin to feel God's love. I believe God's love is ever-present, but we've become detached. For many reasons, we've come to think that love is "out there somewhere." We've come to believe that love is something we have to seek and find. We have to know what love is to experience it. In this book I will help you recognize God's love already present in your life. When your child tells you, "You're the best mommy in the whole world!" that's God's love bouncing off your baby's lips. Yes, I know we hear these words from a six-year-old and think, "He's just trying to manipulate me to get something he wants." But stay with me on this. I'm encouraging you to see how God blesses you through your children. Our children are gifts from God, and in this book we will reflect on how God's love can shine through our parenting.

I particularly want to encourage women to tune in to

God's love—an unconditional, inexhaustible love—because women have struggled with love the most. As wives, we are expected to give emotional support to our husbands. As mothers, we nurture children. In our extended families we get tapped for empathy and sympathy. On our jobs we get called to be the voice of compassion—while men are expected to be the voice of reason. In this book we will reflect on what God says love is, and on what it isn't, so we can find a better balance in our relationships.

As women, we struggle with giving and receiving love. We often give too much and don't expect enough. We think we must earn love—doing favors, buying gifts, giving our all. We think the absence of a boyfriend or husband means we are somehow unworthy of love—or not ready for love, as if love is something we must prepare for. I believe that when we embrace God's love we can find balance in our relationships and avoid the emotional and physical exhaustion we have gotten used to.

In church we accept the popular scripture, "For God so loved the world that he gave his only begotten son, so that whosoever believes in Him shall not perish, but shall have everlasting life." But too often we misinterpret this Scripture (John 3:16). We think, "If God gave His only son, His flesh-and-blood son, then God expects us to give blood, too, right?" Wrong. Women, in particular, have embraced an excessive self-sacrificing love, an idea of love that compels us to try to do too much on any given day. It's like that old

1970s commercial that said, "I can bring home the bacon. Fry it up in a pan. And never, never let you forget you're a man. 'Cause I'm a woman . . ." They were advertising a perfume—and the notion that women can be everything everybody needs her to be. Well, ladies, we do not have to try so hard. We do not have to do so much. God's love doesn't require domestic service 24/7.

These days, we're up at 4:00 a.m. to read the Bible and have a little quiet time with the Lord. By 5:00 we're waking the children to get them dressed for daycare or school. By 6:30 we're out the door on our way to drop off the kids and get to our job. We grab a strong cup of coffee and a sweet muffin to eat at our desk while checking e-mail. We work a demanding eight hours, with meetings and projects to complete. We leave the job at 4:30 to get one child to choir rehearsal and take another to track-and-field practice. By 6:30 p.m. we're back home, serving dinner, while refereeing sibling rivalries. We explain to our spouse why his dry cleaning wasn't dropped off or picked up. We tell Mom—or Auntie or Uncle—we can't talk right now but will try to call them back in a little while. We clean the kitchen, go to bed by ten, get up, and do it all over again.

We work feverishly, catering to what we believe are love's demands. We do this year in and year out for ten to eighteen years and find ourselves depleted. We thought that neglecting any of these duties would mean we're not a good wife, not a good mother, not a good employee, not a good something. In this book, we will examine how God's love can energize rather than exhaust us.

Although the Bible tells us, "God sent his son into the world not to condemn the world, but that the world might be free" (John 3:17), we continue to punish ourselves, carrying guilt from our teens well into our old age. Some women have turned their guilt about having an abortion as a teen into a lifelong mission to "save others" from doing the same. While I believe some of our life experiences can inspire and compel us to lofty endeavors, our efforts should be driven by love, not by guilt. Love doesn't look for our faults and flaws, or hold our past against us. God's love encourages us to be better than we ever thought we could be.

In this book we will take a long, hard look at forgiveness—of self and others. Refusal to forgive is another love-blocker for a lot of women. We will reflect much on what the Bible says about forgiveness, and complete exercises to recognize old grudges and release them. We also will examine another love-blocker: fear of rejection. Many of us carry a painful experience of rejection from our youth into our adult life, maintaining a rejection-consciousness and recreating the experience of rejection again and again. In this book we will look at ways to break the cycle of rejection.

For me, Fear, with a capital "F," was a major barrier to my experiencing God's love in my life. If God's love is like sunshine, I was acting as if I had been sunburned badly and refused to go back to the beach! Imagine fearing the sun because we don't understand it or haven't developed a healthy relationship with it. I had to overcome fear, as many of us do. This book offers exercises to help you overcome the fears that are standing between you and the love God has for you.

Practical Exercises and Journal Prompts

I will encourage you to embrace God's love by developing a personal relationship with Him. I will also show you how to better love yourself, reflecting on what God says about each of us, and taking inventory of the unique qualities, gifts, and talents God has given.

You will find exercises to help you recognize and appreciate the love God already has put in your life; I encourage you to be an expression of God's love too. We will plan ways you can be an expression of God's love where you live, work, pray, and play.

You will be encouraged to meditate on God's words on love—love of self, love of our family, friends, and neighbors, and love of our church community. Each chapter will also include famous quotes about love and grace for your reflection.

Each chapter will conclude with practical applications

for exercising and strengthening your faith, and pages for you to keep a journal of your progress. In her book *Creative Journal Writing: The Art and Heart of Reflection*, author Stephanie Dowrick explains that journaling allows us to discover who we are; it allows us to manage our past and envision a better future. Journaling in these pages can also be your form of prayer and meditation. Tell God what you are feeling and expect for Him to speak to you through the words you write in this journal.

We're used to twenty-one-day challenges, and forty-day fasts. But in this book, I encourage you to slow down a bit. You're invited to enjoy a slow dance with the Holy Spirit. Meditate on the Scripture at the beginning of each chapter. Take time to reflect, for days or weeks, before writing in the journal sections. I am encouraging you to do as I have had to do. Take the pressure off!

Let God's love lift you in His own time, at His own pace. You are free to set timed goals for yourself, of course, but I encourage you to enjoy the process. See how and when your awareness of God's love in your life blossoms. You may focus on a single principle for a week, a month, or a whole year. You may leave some of your journal pages open to record progress in a year, two years, five, ten, or twenty years in the future. In these pages you'll find my own story of being debilitated by fear. God revealed to me the root of my biggest fears, but it took about twenty years for me to work through those fears.

The important thing to remember as you read and work your way through this book is that we cannot put love on a timetable. God loves us. His love is already present in our lives. Our understanding and embracing of His love can happen in a moment of brilliant revelation or sweetly unfold over years. I learned as a psychology major in college that it takes time and effort to break the barriers that block our blessings. I encourage you to seek God's revelations for improving your relationships and enhancing love in your life. I also urge you to do the work to break down your personal barriers. Consider this a labor of love, and enjoy the process. You may want to grab a pack of ink pens in your favorite colors and color-code your work. For instance, you may outline the sentences that resonate most with you in one color, and outline ideas to come back to later in another color. You may choose to journal notes from your present experience in one color and write your updates in other colors leading up to your favorite color. Have fun with this book. Discuss it with your friends, or your book club. Blog about your progress through it. Enjoy!

Invite the Holy Spirit to be with you as you journal. As you begin to reflect on God's love in your relationships, I believe the Holy Spirit will fill you and you will gradually feel better in the relationships you have and the ones you will form.

PART I

Embracing God's Love

GOD MEETS US
WHERE WE ARE

I WAS SITTING IN OUR NEW YORK CHURCH ONE DAY
when the Lord spoke to me and said I should reach out
to women in the entertainment industry. I discussed this
calling with Creflo on our way home that evening, and he
suggested I pray on it. I did. I told God I did not know what
to say or how to reach the women working as exotic dancers
and prostitutes, but God told me to go forward with Holy
boldness and that He would tell me what to say. A team of
women at our church joined me in this ministry, and we have
greeted women in the industry on the streets and talked to
them in their dressing rooms backstage. We go out to the
strip clubs to meet these women where they are, but sometimes they are led to us.

I met a young woman named Tonya through our Prestige outreach ministry, which ministers to women in the sex entertainment industry. Tonya (not her real name) is one of the many women who just needed a little encouragement to begin to see herself the way God sees her.

Tonya started dancing when she was twenty-three years old. As a child, she grew up in an environment where people did whatever they possibly could to earn a living. "I learned to survive on my own," Tonya said. "I didn't have anyone to encourage me, to give me that push. It was hard. My life was a struggle. For instance, it was a challenge for me to get just the basic things I needed. In addition, I was never taught any discipline. I didn't have the love and comfort I needed growing up; therefore, as I grew older I knew that I had to support myself. Dancing in strip clubs was something that I really hated to do, but at the same time, it was quick and fast money, and it got me the things I needed." While working within the sex entertainment industry, Tonya began to realize just how devalued she was. She was treated as if she were a mere object. Patrons would basically use her for their sexual pleasures, and afterward, toss her aside.

One day, a friend of a friend invited Tonya to Bible study at our church, and she attended. As Creflo preached, she understood the Word about God's saving grace. "He even spoke about some things I was feeling at the time," Tonya said. "It really shocked me to hear him speak on the inner battles inside of me—things no one else knew about! I gave my life to the Lord that night. One of the prayer counselors said she was so happy to see me. She said, 'You're the one we've been waiting for.' I thought, 'Wow, it's such a wonderful feeling to know that someone cares, and wants the best for me.' "

Tonya couldn't believe she had been missing out on such a powerful revelation for most of her life. She now believes that because of God's love, she no longer has to devalue herself for money. When she decided to give her life to Christ, Tonya also decided to leave the sex entertainment industry.

Tonya is just one of millions who are discovering their identity in Christ. God wants us to know that we all are cherished in His eyes. Therefore, we should see ourselves the way He sees us, instead of allowing the world to warp and distort our identities. We are God's beloved. He created us in His own image, each with a specific plan and purpose.

As mothers, teachers, aunts, grandmothers, and coworkers, we are in positions to assure others that they are blessed beyond their material treasures, and blessed beyond the fantasies they see on TV. Not only should we tell our daughters that what they see as glamorous and fun in music videos is not reality. We can also remind our peers that what we laugh about on so-called reality TV shows is absolute Hollywood—for entertainment purposes only. We should avoid seeking after what we see on TV. God wants to deliver us all from our fantasies and desires that don't serve Him and don't build His kingdom.

Our Prestige ministry is one of dozens of outreach ministries we have based at our home churches in Atlanta and New York, and through our fellowship churches across the United States and in other countries. Ephesians 5:2 tells us, "Walk in love, as Christ loved us and gave himself up for us, a fragrant offering and sacrifice to God." This requires us to extend God's love beyond the hugs we give in church during our holy welcoming. We want to extend our "fragrance," beyond the perfumes and colognes we wear on Sunday mornings.

Demonstrating God's Love

God tells us how to extend His love and grace in our communities. In the book of Matthew (10:7–8) He tells us, "The kingdom of heaven is at hand. . . . Heal the sick, cleanse the lepers, raise the dead, cast out devils. Freely ye have received, freely give."

God blesses us freely. We don't have to pay God to be blessed. God blesses us without conditions or qualifications. Think about it. We did not pay any money for our ability to see, touch, taste, or hear. God gives these abilities to us freely every day. We did not have to qualify for these blessings. God blesses us because He loves us. We should extend that same love to the people in our lives.

God says in His Word that forgiveness is His habit. That is what He does. We should be quick to forgive. We should be quick to walk in love. Why? Because God already has made these things available to us.

The war is over. We are not believing in, or fearful of, a wrathful God anymore. God delivered us from that in the New Testament. We know now that God is not mad at us. He is not holding anything against us, and we should not hold anything against the people He has put in our lives. Just as God has forgiven us over and over again, we should be quick to forgive.

WHEN WE'RE AT HOME by ourselves, what choices do we make? Do we get into the Word or do we sit in front of the TV? Do we make quality time with God and begin to invest in the relationship that we have with Him? These things are important to do in order to demonstrate the character God wants us to have in our life. Creflo has been teaching our church diligently about demonstrating the character of God. He encouraged everyone to exhibit the fruits of the Holy Spirit in their daily life. He often teaches about the importance of walking in the love of God. The body of Christ has to be a body that's full of character, making the right choices. It's what we do when nobody's looking, when we're not at church that counts most. When we refuse to do what the Word of God says, we put the Word of God to shame. God wants us, as Christians, to demonstrate His character out in the world. God wants us, who love His Word, and believe in His goodness, to begin to attract others through our lifestyle.

God's Love Casts Out Fear

When I was five years old a man came to my bedroom window late one night and scared me half to death. He was tapping on my window to get my attention. He motioned for me to come and open the window. I couldn't hear him through the glass, but his mouth was moving as he leaned in close, waving his hand. I screamed. My father came running into my room, then went and got his shotgun. My father ran out of the house and chased the man off our property. I didn't hear the gun go off, and my father later explained that the man was just a drunk who stumbled into our yard. That stranger at my window traumatized me as a kid, and I felt unsafe most of my life after that.

Early in my Christian walk, when I first began reading the Bible and spending quiet time alone, I realized how full of fear I was. It was a debilitating fear. This fear had me sleeping with the lights on at night, and tucking a chair under the doorknob to keep possible intruders out. Even after I got married, if my husband was away on business I slept with the lights on. And when I became a mother, determined to protect my children, that same fear led to my decision to learn how to handle a gun.

The first time I went to a shooting range, it was with my husband, Creflo, and two of our closest friends. I was excited at the prospect of learning to shoot a gun to protect myself. I was proudly dressed in a tan hunting jacket—full of pockets with nothing in them. When we went into the shooting range, the stench of gunpowder and the fog that filled the air added to my excitement. My friend picked out a very small gun, a .22. It was so cute. I grabbed a huge Uzi.

I was standing there with a pair of goggles on my face and ear protectors over my head, trying to balance a big Uzi on my shoulder. It was the craziest thing. That gun was so powerful, I had to have an attendant standing with me the whole time to make sure I stayed in my lane and aimed straight. This machine gun was very heavy—and hard to shoot—not anything like what I had seen in the movies.

Learning to shoot, I felt like I was doing the right thing. I scaled down from the Uzi and picked up a .357 Magnum. I learned to aim that .357, lining up the red laser dot square on my target, which was a paper outline of a man's torso. I could shoot and hit spot-on at the range. I believed I was supposed to be able to protect my family when my husband was away. Though I was well aware of the dangers of having a gun in the house, I thought that was what God wanted me to do.

One day my teenage son decided to come in the house through one of the side doors that we never use. The alarm went off, making a lot of noise, and I found myself running to get my gun before I realized it was my son. I told him he almost ended up with that red dot on his forehead. We can laugh about it now, but at the time it was frightening to think that I almost shot my son. That's how deeply we can get caught up in fear.

I began to pray and ask God to help me overcome my fear of intruders, my fear of having my personal space violated, my fear of being vulnerable to outside influences—like a stranger tapping at the window in the middle of the night. I read the Scripture (1 John 4:18) that says, "Perfect love casts out all fear," and I began to repeat that Scripture over and over out loud. I would get still sometimes and meditate on that Scripture. Then I began to receive a revelation about fear. The revelation that came to me was that God loves me too much to allow anyone to hurt me. I had to believe that, and let that idea settle into my spirit.

Before my prayer and meditation, I was thinking I had to protect myself all by my own strength. So, I decided to go to a shooting range and learn to shoot. Not that there's anything wrong with learning how to shoot. The problem for me was that my fears had overwhelmed me. Learning to shoot a gun had not made me fearless.

In meditating on God's Word, I began to realize that

God sends angels to protect us, and God's protection is always with us, always in us. For all I know, my father may have been an angel for that drunken man who stumbled onto our property. Facing a shotgun and having to run for his life may have sobered him up long enough for him to get the addiction treatment he needed.

God's ways are not always our ways. His protection may come in the form of a neighbor who notices a stranger lurking about and calls the police in time to catch the would-be burglar. It may come as an instinct that tells us to turn right in a parking lot instead of left. It may be a gut feeling that tells us to check the locks on the patio door.

Traumatic experiences can happen despite our best efforts to avoid them. But knowing that God loves us and that His love is a protective love, allows us to know that even when bad things happen, God can use them for our good. A fear of being assaulted—or an experience of having been assaulted—may lead us to take a martial arts class, where we learn the benefits of mental focus and strength building. When we believe that God's love protects us from harm, we can perceive our frightening experiences differently. Rather than avoiding confrontation, or literally running from a fight, we can face our threats, knowing that win, lose, or draw, we will come out of the confrontation stronger in some way.

Learning that God's perfect love casts out fear compelled me to trust in God's divine protection. God's love gives us peace of mind, and presence of mind. The more I learned to rely on God and trust His Holy Spirit, the less fearful I became.

I still get thoughts of fear some days, particularly when something happens that hits close to home—like a rash of home invasions in our area one year, or the break-in at our oldest daughter's house. But God showed me other ways to manage my fears. God showed me that His love is more powerful and more protective than any weapon man can manufacture or learn to manipulate.

I'm not saying I oppose gun ownership. Many people own guns for protection and for sport. Women, in particular, have been increasingly showing up at shooting ranges and joining shoot and skeet clubs. But I'm trusting God more than guns these days. Like any other mechanical devices, guns can misfire or jam when we need them most. We simply must rely on God for His divine protection. His protection is an expression of His love.

Knowing that God's protection is an expression of His love also means we should expect the men who say they love us to want to protect us. If your fiancé isn't concerned that you're riding the bus halfway across the city after midnight to get home from your job, that should be a red flag for you. If you don't love him enough to pray for his protection when he is in danger, as well, you may certainly want to consider whether you're really committed to caring for him, too. Your sister or girlfriend will ask you to call her when you get home if you are traveling a long distance alone or traveling through dangerous territory. That's an expression of love. When your child is young, you will hold her hand crossing the street to keep her safe. That's your love casting out your child's fear of getting hit by a car.

God's love can cast out fears in any area of our life. Meditate on the Scripture (1 John 4:18), "Perfect love casts out fear," when you're afraid of losing your job, afraid of failing an exam, afraid of disappointing a loved one. God will give you a revelation to ease your anxiety. When you pray for relief from your fear of passing an exam, God may guide you to a new piece of information or a new book that allows you to better prepare for that exam. When you pray about your fear of losing your job, God may remind you of unique talents you have to offer your employer. You may be reminded of a great idea you had years ago that could help your employer achieve new levels of success.

*Wherefore, if God so clothes
the grass of the field . . . shall He
not much more clothe you?*

MATTHEW 6:30

Get to Know God

Webster's dictionary defines love as "affection; kind feeling; friendship; strong liking or desire; fondness; good will." It also says love is "due gratitude and reverence . . ." Love means "to regard with passionate and devoted affection"; also "to take delight or pleasure in; to have a strong liking or desire for, or interest in; to be pleased with; to like." When we become mindful of our affection for God and God's affection for us, we can get a better perspective on our fears. When we are so busy thanking God for what He has given us, we become less afraid of losing a job or a loved one or our material goods. When we delight in knowing God is present in our life, we can become so bright and pleasant that we attract more good people and good experiences to us.

I was marveling at a row of beautiful trees one day in a park. Just staring at the trees, God gave me understanding about the beauty of His creation. He gave me a greater appreciation for our uniqueness, too. I noticed that the oak tree and the willow seemed to get along peacefully. The willow wasn't bent over, trying to make the oak more like it. And the oak wasn't tussling with the willow to bring it into submission. They stood tall in their own space, doing what God designed trees to do—clean the air and give shade. I thanked God for my walk in the park that day, and thanked

Him for bringing my attention to one of the many lessons He has planted all around us. I was reminded of what the Bible tells us in Matthew 6:30–34: "Wherefore, if God so clothes the grass of the field . . . shall He not much more clothe you? Therefore take no thought of what you will eat or drink. . . . Your heavenly father knows that you need these things. . . . But put God first and all these things will be given to you."

God wants us to have a relationship with Him first— and in our heart of hearts, we want a relationship with Him, too. We yearn to be connected to something. In our mother's womb we were connected. During our formative years we relied on someone bigger than us to feed us, buy us clothes, and provide for all our basic needs. We have an innate desire to feel connected. I believe God wants us to acknowledge our connection to Him. He wants us to be mindfully connected to Him first and foremost. We connect to God by spending time reading His Holy Scriptures. We connect by praying, telling Him what's in our heart and on our mind. We connect by meditating, listening, expecting to hear His guidance for our lives. We connect to God when we acknowledge His presence, when fellowshipping and giving praise at church. We commune with God when we appreciate His wonders in nature, too.

We get to know God on a more intimate level by spending time with Him. God wants us to spend time with Him, but He doesn't want us to think of it as an obligation. He wants us to delight in our time with Him. Even if we don't feel like spending time with Him, we can ask Him to help us by giving us the desire to spend time with Him. By His grace, He will give us the desire to spend time with Him. So many people grew up feeling obligated to go to church, and as soon as they were out on their own they wanted nothing more to do with church. Church for them had become a religious chore, a Sunday sacrifice of sorts. But they believed if they didn't go to church every Sunday—and to Bible study and choir rehearsal during the week—surely they would go to hell when they died. God wants our church experience, our fellowship with other believers, our collective worship to be delightful. I encourage people to find the church that's right for them. Ask God to guide you.

Once we yield ourselves to God, He leads us into His power, ability, and strength. Being in tune with God will allow us to experience His love in small gestures and grand experiences. Remember the singing group the Spinners? They gave us the R & B hit "Mighty Love." *Keep on loving. You'll soon discover, a mighty love.* They sang it with so much soul. I believe God's love is the mightiest love. And when we understand how God expresses His love, we can recognize His love in our life. Knowing what to look for, we will discover love in the relationships we have with the people in our life.

There is therefore now no condemnation to them which are in Christ Jesus, who walk not after the flesh, but after the Spirit.

ROMANS 8:1

God's Love Is Unconditional

I heard of an elderly woman, Iris, who was a deaconess in a small church in a big city. This woman, in her late eighties, was very old-fashioned and conservative. She was so conservative that even in the twenty-first century she refused to wear pants to church. The church, in fact, was so conservative, that the deaconesses were not allowed to sit in the front pews during communion. These women church leaders had to sit behind the men. They believed in the old traditions more than anything.

One day Iris noticed that one of the young women singing in the choir was pregnant. The young woman was not married, and it offended Iris to see her singing in the choir. "Her mouth might be saying one thing on Sunday mornings, but her body was saying something else on Saturday night," Iris whispered to a woman sitting next to her. Deaconess Iris told the pastor and deacon board that the young woman should be "called down front" and made an example of. Iris believed the young woman should be condemned before the entire congregation, to show the other young people in the church that sin was not acceptable. Thankfully, the compassion of others prevailed and the young woman was not called to account. Four years later, that young woman's daughter delighted the congregation with a stirring recitation of the books of the Bible at their Resurrection (Easter) celebration. At four years, the child, born out of wedlock, could name all the books of the Bible with remarkable delivery. She was bright and charming onstage. Another Sunday, she recited poet Maya Angelou's classic poem "Still I Rise" with such drama she brought the congregation to their feet.

The young mother, once shunned by Deaconess Iris and others in the church, taught the little girl another poem to recite at Iris's birthday in the fellowship hall at the church.

"I'm not cute or built to suit a fashion model's size," the little girl recited with all the drama her three-foot frame could project. "But when I start to tell them, / They think I'm telling lies . . . I'm a woman / Phenomenally. / Phenomenal woman, / That's me."

As the little girl confidently recited the lengthy poem, "Phenomenal Woman," also by Angelou, the audience marveled at her remarkable memory. Deaconess Iris could not hold back her tears. She embraced the little girl and told everyone the little girl would be her adopted granddaughter.

God shined His unconditional love through a little girl in a church to remind church folk in the twenty-first century that love is unconditional. God gifted her with remarkable talents, regardless of who her parents were, regardless of when and how she was conceived. God shined His love through this little girl even in the absence of her father.

As Christians, we celebrate the miraculous virgin

birth of Jesus every year. We thank God His mother had the courage to keep the pregnancy although she would be shunned as an unwed mother. But too often we don't extend that admiration of courage and appreciation of the miracle of birth to the people in our lives. God tells us in Romans 8:1 that "There is no condemnation for those who are in Christ."

In the Old Testament, we see people living under a judgmental covenant. Imperfect people were labeled and shunned. A person with a missing limb was not allowed to join the other church folk at the altar. If you were labeled crippled or crazy you were not welcomed in the church. Church folk believed that if you were not whole, you could not stand before God. They believed an ordained minister had to sacrifice an animal for God to bless you. But even the sacrificial animal had to be without blemish. But in the New Testament, we learn otherwise. In the New Testament, God tells us He loves us unconditionally.

In the New Testament, Luke 7:36–50, tells us that Jesus loved and honored even the women everyone else condemned. Luke tells us Jesus is having a meal in the home of a Pharisee named Simon. Luke says a "sinful" woman from the city arrived to meet Jesus with an alabaster box of ointment. She stood behind Jesus and wept. Her tears washed his feet. She kneeled down and used her hair to wipe his feet. Simon, seeing their interaction, asked Jesus, "Don't you know she's a sinner?" To which Jesus replied, "When I came in, you did not offer me water for my feet. But this woman washed my feet with her tears, and wiped them with her hair. When I came in, you did not embrace me. But this woman has not stopped embracing me. You did not offer me oil for my head. But this woman did."

Imagine that. Here is Jesus—God personified, our perfect, flawless Savior—allowing a sinful woman to touch Him. Jesus saw the woman for who she was. He appreciated the love offerings she gave. He did not even ask about her past.

Some people don't bother to attend church anymore because they have been betrayed, judged, taken advantage of, accused, or abused by fellow Christians. I encourage people to understand that Christians are not Christ reincarnated. We strive to be like Christ, but we are human, and must be born again. Christ was human *and* divine. Many of us in the church have good intentions, but our actions do not truly reflect the heart of God. That is why I appreciate the ministry of Jesus. He didn't take a religious approach to saving the lost. In fact, religious people hated Him because He didn't condemn people. Jesus was compassionate. He was forgiving. He healed rather than hurt people. He demonstrated God's unconditional love.

Can you imagine how much happiness we would all experience if we ceased to judge others, ceased to try to change people, and ceased to try to punish them for their actions? Visualize celebrating the differences in others, rather than condemning. For instance, if you have a friend who is always late, ask her to come an hour early to help with something, knowing that your request may get her there right on time.

God Forgives

Humans have suffered feelings of guilt and shame since the beginning of time, ever since Adam and Eve ate the forbidden fruit. They tried to hide from God out of shame. God has since taught us about forgiveness. The Word says, "There is therefore now no condemnation to them which are in Christ Jesus, who walk not after the flesh, but after the Spirit" (Romans 8:1).

The word *condemnation* means "to judge or declare unfit for use." Feelings of condemnation steal our confidence and rob us of courage and boldness. But God's love gives us confidence and boldness. All of us have made mistakes in life, and many of us tend to dwell on those imperfections. I think of the young girls who got pregnant out of wedlock, who want to accept God's forgiveness but cannot because people in the church have made them feel condemned. I think of young women suffering domestic violence, feeling they have no way out, no choice but to stay with their abuser. I think of the thousands of women who think that God is angry with them for having abortions. They believe that God is holding their sins against them. But God's Word teaches us otherwise.

"I have sworn not to be angry with you, never to rebuke you again. Though the mountains be shaken and the hills be removed, yet my unfailing love for you will not be shaken nor my covenant of peace be removed," says the Lord in Isaiah 54:9–10, NIV.

Many women have internalized a lot of pain, shame, and blame because of the judgment of others. Creflo and I have encountered and counseled a host of women with scenarios like the ones I've mentioned, which is why we have become so passionate about teaching the grace of Jesus Christ.

We all make mistakes, and we all have flaws. But we have to fight the urge to wallow in self-pity and guilt when we miss the mark. If ten years ago you stole your best friend's boyfriend—or husband—you don't have to spend the rest of your life worried that you are, deep down inside, untrustworthy. You don't have to worry that the law of karma is waiting to come and snatch your man away. God didn't say we would not have consequences for our actions, but He doesn't want you to live the rest of your life in guilt and shame. God's love moves us to make amends, seek forgiveness, and move on. God wants us to forgive ourselves.

You may have regretted that you were too busy working hard, making money, to take time off and help care for your mother in her final years. If you talk to God about it, He may reveal to you that He took care of your mother's needs better than you knew. You may meet one of her former neighbors who will tell you of some wonderful experiences your mother enjoyed before she died. Being in a relationship with God, talking to Him, studying His words—these things deliver us from regrets.

God does not condemn us, although He does correct us. He is not looking for opportunities to punish us or make us feel bad about ourselves. He is not a God who is constantly punishing us each time we do something wrong. Because He loves us, we should love ourselves. When we recognize that we are being critical of ourselves, we should take inventory of what we have been hearing and speaking about ourselves, and make changes as necessary.

We can change the company we keep and avoid those who would speak discouraging comments to us. We can change our language to reflect who we would like to become rather than repeat our mistakes and bad experiences from the past. Instead of saying, "I got fired because they accused me of stealing money," we can say, "I've had some circumstances that showed me it's not enough to just be trustworthy. I need to make sure other people know I'm honest. I've got a lot of integrity, but I may not have been making that clear before." Of course, if you really stole money and repented, God forgave you the moment you repented, and you would be wise to be diligent in the future about avoiding temptations to steal.

If we have been around negative influences, we can make a quality decision to limit—or eliminate, if necessary—those influences. If you had a problem with addiction in the past, you don't have to live the rest of your life ashamed and guilty. God may use your insights to help others avoid it.

Because he holds fast to me in love,
I will deliver him; I will protect him,
because he knows my name.

Psalms 91:14

God Redeems

Jaleesa, age forty-three, realized she was overcompensating for an injustice done to her when she was a young woman. She often put on a hard-core demeanor to let people know she would not be taken advantage of again. "I've adopted this attitude that no one is going to hurt me again. I am determined not to be a weak woman who allows people to walk all over me," she said.

At nineteen, Jaleesa fell in love with a man who was ten years her senior. He seemed kindhearted and skilled in counseling others. He helped her to deal with the sexual abuse she had encountered as a child. He helped her deal with being angry with her abusers, and with her mother. She had felt hurt because certain men in her family would take her affection for them and turn it into something sexual. She also questioned her mother's decision to leave her alone with her boyfriend when she was only eleven years old. She never understood why her mother did that, and she resented her for that, but she never told anyone about her resentment.

Jaleesa thought she had found a man who cared for her. He was intelligent, insightful, but she later discovered he was also an atheist. By the time she found out about his religious beliefs, she was already in love with him and decided their religious differences shouldn't matter. She had been raised in a Christian home but never studied the Bible and knew little about the ramifications of an individual's religion.

Jaleesa felt her new love was someone she could confide in, and that was all that mattered at the time. He did show signs of being controlling, but Jaleesa saw the control as a sign of his affection. A year into the relationship, she became pregnant. When she shared the news with her boyfriend, he became angry and wanted her to have an abortion immediately.

He was adamant about it. He didn't want to have children. But Jaleesa didn't want to have an abortion. She had already abandoned some of her beliefs for the sake of their relationship. She would spend Sunday mornings cuddling with him instead of going to church, and that seemed all right. But when she was faced with having an abortion, which she opposed as a Christian, she resisted. In her family, growing up, abortion was never an option. Her family believed if God blessed you to get pregnant, God would make provisions to raise the child. But in the end Jaleesa gave in to her boyfriend's demands.

Jaleesa's boyfriend drove her to the clinic as she silently cried all the way there. She couldn't believe her boyfriend had *no* sympathy for how she felt about the situation. He didn't even go inside the clinic with her. She had to face it all alone. He seemed cold and indifferent, as if he didn't even have a conscience.

Jaleesa ended the relationship soon afterward and never

told anyone about the abortion. But several months later, around the time she would have given birth, she became angry with herself for not having stood up to her boyfriend. She believed she had been a weak woman, and she hated herself for that. She would carry that anger and shame for many years.

Jaleesa decided to give God a try again and joined a church. One day she heard her pastor preach about God's love, and finally she understood. She was able to heal because of the revelations she received about the love of God and His forgiveness. Going to a church where the Word was being taught with simplicity and clarity made a huge difference. It helped her understand that God was not holding anything against her because of that decision to get an abortion. That revelation alone helped her forgive herself.

Jesus Christ makes us new. That simply means we no longer have to identify with our sin because we can begin to identify with Him. Therefore, we no longer have to allow the enemy to beat us up, making us feel guilty and condemned over some bad decision or situation from the past. God has decided not to remember those sins anymore because of what His son has done. Now, *that's* love!

Isaiah 1:18 says, " 'Come now, let's settle this,' says the Lord. 'Though your sins are like scarlet, I will make them as white as snow. Though they are red like crimson, I will make them as white as wool.' " I find it so amazing that when we become born-again Christians, our spirits become pure. They are so pure that the Holy Spirit can dwell there. That's truly amazing.

When we really begin to grasp the reality of the person of the Holy Spirit dwelling within us, we will begin to sense His presence in various ways. When we sense His presence, we can't help but sense His love. For example, you may have a "gut" feeling or a strong inclination that you should do something, and not even be aware that it is the Holy Spirit leading you and guiding you. Well, guess what? Not only will He lead and guide your life, He will also heal your broken heart when someone has hurt you. He helps us to forgive ourselves and understand how to do things His way. This is the way we begin to embrace all that He is. We begin to see Him as an actual person, and the only difference is we can't see Him.

Like Jaleesa, many women are dealing with feelings of guilt and condemnation because of decisions they've made in the past. Actually, we have all made unwise decisions that we regret. But should we beat ourselves up over those decisions? Absolutely not! I want to encourage any woman who has had an abortion, experienced teen pregnancy, or any other life-altering experience, to realize that there is no condemnation if you belong to Jesus Christ! Refuse to allow the devil to keep beating you up with his lies. Embrace who you are because of Christ, and because of the love of God that is constantly demonstrated through His grace.

*Grace and peace be multiplied
to you in the knowledge of God
and of Jesus our Lord.*

2 PETER 1:2

God's Love Is Graceful

One young woman I work with in our church told me how her understanding of God's love delivered her from feeling unwanted. Kate, who you will hear more from in a later chapter, lost both of her parents at a young age. Growing up an orphan, she felt unwanted. But as a young woman she began reading her Bible. She gained hope through stories about others who had experienced a change in fortune. She read about Esther, who had also been orphaned. Esther was raised by her uncle. She, too, must have felt abandoned at times. She, too, must have wondered why God took both of her parents. Esther must have cried many nights wondering what would become of her. But when Esther was a young woman, she was introduced to a king. The king fell in love with her and made her his queen.

Esther did not have the same pedigree as the other women presented to the king. She did not have the impressive dowry some of the other women likely had. She did not have the confidence of a young woman raised by loving, doting parents. But the king chose her. The Bible tells us, "After you have suffered for a little while, the God of all grace . . . will Himself perfect, confirm, strengthen and establish you" (1 Peter 5:10).

God's grace is what gives us unmerited favor. The dictionary defines *grace* as "divine love bestowed freely on people." As we get in a relationship with God, we can expect to experience His grace in our life. We may not all marry a king, but we will learn to appreciate the kinglike qualities of the people already in our life.

"God told me to 'abide in Him,'" Kate said. "When I looked to others for my fulfillment, I began to lose my true identity as a Christian. There were times when I felt that absolutely no one loved or cared for me, but He has shown me His amazing love. Through His grace, He has shown me how to be the best 'me' I can be. Even though people may not always accept me, I know that I'm accepted in Him. I am not easily offended anymore. I simply see people through the eyes of grace. I don't hold anything against anyone anymore."

As Kate became less bitter, she became friendlier, offering God's grace to others through a friendly smile.

Like Kate, I too had to overcome some insecurities. I did not have the traditional formal training in theology, but God was calling me to minister and co-pastor our expanding church. I was terrified about getting up and speaking. But I had to trust that if God called me to do it, He would give me whatever I needed to fulfill this calling. Finally, I had to realize that God already had equipped and empowered me to speak the truths He assigned for me to speak.

I love Marvin Sapp's song "The Best in Me." It reminds me that God sees my intentions even when others are focused only on outcomes and are measuring me by their own standards of success. When I set my intentions to speak God's

Holy Word, I had to decide I would speak it wherever God sent me to speak. I would speak it in our churches in Atlanta and New York. I would speak it in communities across the country and around the globe. I decided I would speak to large crowds of thousands gathered at women's conferences or to the few hundred people who show up at our church on Friday morning for a workshop. I want to encourage you to believe that God sees the best in you. God sees your intentions, your efforts. God sees your beauty, your talent. God sees your resilience and fortitude. If you don't have a parent, someone in your extended family, or a lifelong friend who has always seen the best in you, be still and know that God sees the best in you.

Exercises

OPENING PRAYER

Heavenly Father, I thank You for Your Word today. Father, I thank You for Your all-providing, all-protecting, ever-abiding love and grace in my life. Father, I open my hearts to You today, accepting the love You have already given me.

Here are a few things you can do to reengage your love affair with God.

1. **MAKE A LIST**

   One of the ways we can actively experience God's love is by believing that we already have it. *Make a list of what God has already given you, beginning with life itself. Add to your list each day until you become so aware of God's love in your life that you don't have to think about it, that you wake up daily thanking Him for loving you in His many ways.*

2. **ASK GOD**

   Ask God to reveal to you the many ways He already has loved you—and write down what He reveals. Keep this as a note to yourself. Carry it in your wallet or record it in your diary.

3. **LIVE LOVE**

   Let God's love shine through you daily in a smile, a kind word, a favor, or a pardon.

4. **SPEAK IT**

   We should recognize that God's power, His love, and His faith is greater than that which is in the world. *Affirm daily in the mirror, in your diary, or to a dear friend: "Greater is He that is in me than he that is in the world."*

5. **PRAY**

   Remember, nothing about you is too small or insignificant for God. He is a friend that sticks closer than any brother. He wants to be our closest and dearest friend. We can talk to Him just as we talk to our friends and loved ones. And the best part is, He's never unavailable. He is always waiting with open arms to hear about everything concerning us. *Talk to God daily.*

Journal Questions/Prompts

1. What is your favorite Bible verse regarding God's love for us? Why do you like this particular verse most?

2. What is your favorite way to spend time with God?

3. Finish this sentence: "If I believed back then that God really loved me I would not have . . ."

4. Complete this sentence: "One thing I can stop doing now that I am reminded that God loves me uncondi-tionally is . . ."

Initial thoughts

Breakthrough

Growth

More Growth

Practice of New Understanding

Mastery of New Understanding

PART II

A Loving You

You are altogether beautiful, my love;
there is no flaw in you.

SONG OF SOLOMON 4:7

At My Wit's End
I Found God

I WAS SORT OF A REBEL GROWING UP. BY THE TIME I was eighteen, I had grown out of control. Boys found me attractive in my always bold and bright colors. But inside I was a raging storm. I drank and popped pills in my bedroom right next to my parents' room. I partied and smoked marijuana. But I was discreet about it, so no one in my household really knew.

I went to good schools. I was bused to Northside High in Atlanta, where they specialized in the performing arts. I was a majorette in the marching band there. After high school, I went to North Carolina A&T in Greensboro. That transition was a little difficult because it was an HBCU (that is, one of America's historically black colleges and universities), and I had gone to predominantly white schools. The HBCU was kind of a culture shock.

I also didn't like being so far away from my family when I went to college. On top of all that, I was worried because my parents were talking about getting a divorce. My time at A&T was probably the darkest time in my life. I had no purpose. Drugs didn't do anything for me anymore. When I came down off a high, I still had to deal with myself. I had been on that same roller-coaster ride all through high school. Enough was enough. August to January of my first year was really bad, and I left A&T after one semester and enrolled in West Georgia College, which was closer to home.

Meanwhile, I was in a long-distance relationship with a guy in the military, and he wanted to get married. He was charming, and good-looking, but it seemed like every time I was with him, something weird happened. One time when I was visiting him out of town, he got arrested for shoplifting and I had to figure out how to get myself home. I realized that relationship wasn't going to work out, but the pending breakup stressed me out. I cried a lot back in my dorm room. I felt devastated. I was trying to figure out what to do next. I felt as if I were coming to the end of myself.

Around this time, someone in my dorm told me about a Bible study group. She was handing out fliers, and gave me one. I read it and saw that the Bible study was being led by a man named Creflo. Creflo? I thought this would be some old white guy trying to teach a bunch of young people. Still,

I considered going, because maybe it would take my mind off other things. A few days later a friend of mine told me about this same Bible study group. Over the next couple of weeks, I heard several other people around campus talking about it. Finally my interest was piqued.

Bible study would be new for me. Growing up, my parents had not taken us to church much. We went about twice a year, on holidays. I decided maybe God was what I was missing in my life. One day I joined my friend and some of the others from our dorm who were going to the Bible study meeting. It was held in a large conference room in another dormitory hall. People were singing praise songs. Then the man named Creflo got up to teach at the front of the room. Within seconds, I said to my friend, "Now, that's the type of guy I'd want to be my husband." I wanted to marry him, or someone just like him. He was different from the other guys I had met. He demonstrated strength and character. And I thought he was very handsome.

He wasn't just reading the Bible and giving us a bunch of theoretical stuff. He applied it to real life. It was a very powerful experience. He was making God real for me. Immediately afterwards, I literally ran back to my dorm room, I was so excited about what I learned in Bible study. I got down on my knees right then and there and prayed the prayer that was on the flier. It was a simple prayer, real short, but it was powerful.

I prayed, "Heavenly Father, come into my life and save

me. I believe Jesus died for me." I felt different immediately. I knew right then and there that I was changed. It was the weirdest thing. In the days after that, I didn't want another drink. I didn't want another smoke. I didn't want anything but to spend time with God. That was all. I knew without a shadow of a doubt that I wasn't the same person anymore. I just knew.

I officially broke up with my military boyfriend. I didn't want to fornicate. I no longer found it necessary. I felt like I found what I had been missing all my life. It was a sense of peace and unconditional love. I was baffled by what I'd found. I began to soak it all in. I wanted to understand God more and have a personal relationship with Him.

Growing up, we had not read the Bible in my home. I had not gotten that whole "God thing." But now it was all beginning to make sense to me. I became a Christian and began reading the Bible every day. I would pray, and I would read certain Scriptures out loud. I continued to go to Bible study on campus and met a lot of fellow students who were trying to learn as much as I was.

When I went home to visit one weekend, my parents were watching Billy Graham on television. It was an interesting coincidence. I sat down and watched with them. They had recently worked through the problems in their relationship. We ended up talking about needing to be born again. They both prayed and accepted Jesus into their lives at the end of the program, before my very eyes. Over the next few months, I began to see my mother's life totally change. She began going to church and Bible study. Eventually, both of my brothers became born-again Christians, and one of them would become a minister. We all became fully devoted to our new relationship with God.

When I returned to college, we would have Bible study at Creflo's mother's house on the weekends, or in the basement of the church where he was a member. I watched Creflo baptize students in a swimming pool. I began working with Creflo and the others in our Bible study group's street team. We did a lot of recruiting and outreach. Alone in my dorm room, I read the Bible and Bible reference books.

I read all I could about the Virtuous Woman and wanted to become one-hundred-percent renewed. I began to change my wardrobe and dress less seductively. I wanted to get everything right, right away. It would take years, though, for me to understand that God loved me—flaws and all. It would also take years for me to accept myself—flaws and all.

After years of self-destructive intoxication, God gave me an authentic exhilaration, which felt so much better. Praising God and working with the Bible study group was exciting—without the guilt I had after partying and getting drunk or high. Once I became sober and born again, I began to see myself as a purposeful person, an honorable person. I felt good about myself. I *liked* myself!

Still, I was putting a lot of pressure on myself to be

everything the Bible said a virtuous woman should be. Proverbs 31 said the virtuous woman is trustworthy. I knew I could be trusted. Check. It said a virtuous woman would do her husband good, no evil. I didn't have a husband yet, but I was sure that when I became a wife I could do my husband some good. So, again, check. It said a virtuous woman seeks wool and flax and works with her hands. Now, that's where I started to have doubts. I could wear wool sweaters, but flax? At nineteen years old, I didn't even know what flax was.

The Bible said a virtuous woman "will bring food from afar." And so I was wondering whether Taco Bell could be considered "afar." Was I supposed to learn to cook and take food to Bible study or something? I really wanted to get it right. It would take years for me to realize God doesn't expect us to be everything, or do everything—certainly not all at once. But I didn't know this at the time. I was thinking, "The virtuous woman made her own clothes? And she made them out of silk? I can't afford silk! And I don't know how to sew. But, my mom sewed. So maybe I can learn to sew." Proverbs 31 said that when she talks, she sounds wise and kind. I was thinking, "I could do that—maybe. But give me a few more years. Maybe I will be wise by the time I finish college."

I continued to read the Bible and reflect on what I read. When I read Song of Solomon 4:7—"You are altogether beautiful, there is no flaw in you"—a sudden peace came over me. I began to understand that God wanted me. I began to love myself as I was, flaws and all. I was not going to beat myself up because of my past behavior. God said I was beautiful, and I began telling myself that. My past behavior was a reflection of self-hate, not self-love.

Drug and alcohol addictions are not the only indications of low self-esteem or self-hate. Self-hate shows up as jealousy, envy, lying, even overeating. When we are speaking ill of others, it is often because we don't feel good about our own lives. We criticize a woman in a powerful position, for instance, because we wish we were in her position. We look for every flaw we can find to try to bring her down to our level. We criticize the young woman who had a baby out of wedlock, secretly wishing we had had the courage to keep a baby we let our boyfriend talk us into aborting. We bad-mouth the shapely woman in a stunningly attractive outfit not only because she has the curves we wish we had, but— "How dare she have the nerve to strut her stuff!" I'm not advocating wearing a catsuit to the office; every outfit has its place. What I am saying is that we have to look at each other with more love, less envy. The next time you find yourself criticizing someone else, ask yourself, "What's really going on here?" Find something nice to say about the person you've been criticizing. God made each of us, and God loves each of us. When we practice seeing the good in others, we begin to expect that others will see the good in us, too. As we become less fearful that others are focused on our faults, we become free to give and receive love.

For decades now, I've been speaking to women on the importance of loving themselves. I want to encourage you to find your true self—*your* thoughts rather than your parents' thoughts, or your husband's, or your friends' thoughts. I encourage you to look within and acknowledge your truest feelings and identify and understand your motivations. I want to encourage you to release the pressure you may be placing on yourself, and begin to realize that God loves you just as you are.

Consider a conversation you could have with God about you as His personal product. God is clearly proud of His accomplishment, having created you. He made you with flesh and blood and gave you life. He gave you all five senses and the use of all your body parts. He even made you funny, or wise, or extraordinarily caring. He's proud. He looks at you and smiles. But He hears you falsely advertising His product daily. He hears you telling people, "I'm so stupid. I can't believe I made that mistake." He hears you say, "Nobody ever listens to me. I might as well keep my mouth shut." He hears you say, "I'm just lucky to be here." God loves us better than we love our most prized possession. If your diamond bracelet could talk, even if it said, "I know you don't want me anymore now that I fell in the mud because the latch broke," you would say, "But you're diamonds, and you're mine!" God loves us more than that!

Virtuous Isn't Vice-Free

I like to meditate on what it means to be a virtuous woman. Proverbs 31:10–31 tells us much about the virtuous woman, and I believe that it's time for women to begin to appreciate God's virtue in our lives. Being virtuous is not about behaving like a Miss Goody Two-Shoes. It's about knowing your worth, knowing your God, getting power and results through your faith. We want to see results manifesting in our lives. We want to be better individuals, better daughters, sisters, and friends as a result of our reading the Word and applying the wisdom God reveals to us.

I've heard from women who felt somewhat frustrated by reading Proverbs 31. I felt the same way initially. I was thinking, "I can be trustworthy and kind and help my husband in his work. But, God, I don't know how to sew to make our clothes; and I can cook a meal, but you're asking me to get up in the middle of the night and go slay an animal to get the meat? God, I can't do that!" I read, "She considers a field, and buys it. With the fruit of her hands she plants a vineyard." I was thinking, "God, I make a pretty good fruit salad for my family sometimes. But I'm not a farmer, not even inclined to plant a garden."

I learned that there's a process that God wants to see in our lives. When I went back and meditated on this Scripture,

I found that this was a woman who was in a kind of labor. This was a woman who was in distress and bringing forth things. God has something to bring forth in all our lives. God understands what needs to take place in our lives and He's given us his Word to meditate on so we can begin to conceive those possibilities.

As we look at God's Word, we should see ourselves in it and begin to reflect on how God sees us. God says in Proverbs 31:10, "A virtuous woman is worth more than rubies." We want to begin to understand that this is how God sees us. I am not suggesting a narcissistic mindset. Don't go standing in the mirror in your bedroom with your hand on your hip, giving attitude, like, "Yeah, I'm all that because God says I am!" I am suggesting that we take a close look at the values God has instilled in us and appreciate those values. If you happen to be an outspoken, boisterous woman by nature but you secretly wish you were not because you were teased about being "unladylike," begin to appreciate the courage God gave you to speak up and speak out. If you happen to be a soft-spoken woman, privately wishing you were more outspoken, I encourage you to embrace the quiet strength God invested in you. We reflect God's virtues by being authentic, fully embracing our uniqueness.

As we look in the mirror of God's Word and naturally make adjustments in our thinking, we will begin to see adjustments in our behavior, and those adjustments will transform our life. A virtuous woman is a woman of ability, a woman of might, a woman of strength, a woman of the anointing. A virtuous woman brings joy to her home. A woman of virtue is a woman who knows how to put what she reads in the Bible into operation in every area of her life. I encourage you to go beyond buying the cute little necklace with the crucifix, or posting your favorite prayers all around your cubicle at work. That's all very nice, but we have to put these beliefs in our walk. My prayer for you is that you get revelation from God, and that it improves your life. I believe it's impossible to spend time with God and not become transformed. I pray that you will be transformed from the inside out.

The pain, the heartache, the disappointment, or whatever situation you may have faced in the past can be turned around to your favor. By getting a hold of God's Word, you will find your mourning turning into joy.

I encourage you to read Proverbs 31 over and over, as the Word of God continues to give birth to more and more revelation. God's Word is so fresh, it's so full of truth, that it will bring forth for you a burst of revelation like you've never seen before. There's a work that God wants to do in our lives that will cause us to forget about our past and to begin to expect God for the new wonderful experiences.

*Hear the instruction of your
father, and reject not nor forsake the
teaching of your mother. For they are a
victor's garland of grace upon your
head and chains and pendants of gold
worn by kings for your neck.*

PROVERBS 1:8–9

Be All You Can Be—For God

I've always studied radical, amazing women: First Lady Eleanor Roosevelt, Mary McLeod Bethune, and Harriet Tubman—especially Harriet Tubman. I was amazed at how she was guided by God to freedom. She couldn't read, didn't have a map, much less a GPS. There were no road signs, no directions. She just went day to day, guided by God. Not only did she gain her freedom, she went back and freed hundreds more.

For ten years, she went back and forth, running through dark forests, wading through murky swamps, trusting people she was directed to for shelter on what became known as the Underground Railroad. She was divinely guided. One biographer, Beverly Lowry, said Harriet began having visions after she sustained a deep wound to her head when she was thirteen years old. She had been hit in the head by a lead weight thrown at a runaway slave near where she was standing. After suffering that head injury, she would occasionally black out in the middle of a conversation; afterwards she would tell of visions she had received during these momentary blackouts. She told of visions of being helped across a fence to freedom.

She "began having visions and speaking with God on a daily basis, as directly and pragmatically as if He were a guardian uncle whispering instructions exclusively to her and in the most concrete terms about what to do and what not to do, where to go and where not to go," Lowry notes in her book *Harriet Tubman: Imagining a Life*.

Our lady Moses (a nickname of Tubman's) had a deep, abiding longing for freedom and a powerful sense for justice. She trusted her instinct. She told of "a fluttering in her heart" that warned her of impending danger. She had learned from her father to pay attention to her night dreams and daytime visions. She had learned to be confident in her understanding of her dreams and visions.

I believe confidence is an expression of love, and I encourage you to raise your level of confidence in God. Confidence in God surpasses self-confidence. When we root ourselves in a consciousness of God's love for us, we open ourselves up to God's supernatural abilities. Being self-confident may have allowed Harriet Tubman to escape. She may have had the strength and courage to run away from the plantation one night. But being grounded in God, she received supernatural courage from Him, and through God she delivered thousands. Believe in the dreams God puts in your heart.

Reading about Harriet Tubman in college encouraged me. I still draw inspiration from her. Knowing that after leading slaves to freedom in northern states and Canada she served as a Union spy, an Army scout, and a nurse and cook during the Civil War, encourages me to keep going. I love speaking and inspiring women in churches and at church events these days. But I am excited about all that God can do through me in the future as well. I encourage you to get excited about all that God can do through you, too.

You may be a teacher today. But who knows? God may see you as a principal in the future. God may have an educational game for you to design, a program that will teach millions of children around the world. God may compel you to write a series of children's books, inspired by your students. I encourage you to talk to God, and let Him know you're available and willing. Listen for His instructions. Understand how God speaks to you. For Harriet Tubman it was through dreams and visions, through a voice she understood clearly. God speaks to me through revelations. I study, read, and meditate on the Word and gain clarity about what to do and what not to do. Listen for God's guidance in your life.

As you become confident in your relationship with God, you will become confident in your actions, and your confidence will become a beautiful expression of God's love in your life.

Become Battle Ready

Sometimes when we're alone, single, we spend all our time praying to be in a relationship. God may have put you in a place of solitude for a season so He can train you up all over again. In the military, individuals train for upcoming battles. They have a daily regimen of eating balanced meals, building strength, and building stamina. In their training they become single-minded about their preparation for battle. Likewise, we have to train ourselves for the life we want. Just like military soldiers train for combat, we must prepare to battle the enemies who would block us from feeling God's love. Envy is an enemy that will block you from experiencing the love God has already put in your life. Envy will keep you from experiencing greater measures of love God already has in store for you.

You may be home alone one night, crying to God: "God, it's not fair. I've been celibate the past four years, keeping myself chaste and ready for my Godly man. But You brought Sister So-and-so a Godly man to marry, and she's not even saved! God, it's just not fair." Envy may be whispering to you, "You're the one who's been keeping God's commandments, going to church four nights a week. How come you didn't get the reward?" Let me stop you right there. God may be calling you to deal with your issue of envy and comparison.

God may have set you still in order for you to train your mind to a new way of thinking. God may have set you still, in a quiet place, home alone so you can read, study, and meditate on His word. God may have given you alone time to get to know yourself better. What movies do you like? Why? What makes you happy? What makes you sad? What makes you feel energized? What makes you feel drained?

What are you arming yourself with—spiritually? When life's challenges come—and they will—you want your mind to respond on automatic pilot: "Though I walk through the valley of the shadow of death, I will fear no evil. God is with me. God comforts me."

You want to be ready if the doctor says, "I'm sorry to tell you this, but you have a life-threatening disease." If you've done your training, your mind and body, hopefully, are conditioned to respond, "But God has told me it is well with my soul." Obviously, after you get over the shock and devastation, you are prepared to proceed with the necessary treatment and life changes to become healthy again. When Creflo was diagnosed with prostate cancer, and I prayed for his total recovery and healing, he fought back with prayer and fasting, and laughter. He kept his itinerary, and even kept his scheduled appointment to appear on comedian Rickey Smiley's TV show, where he knew he would have fun and could enjoy good humor. Proverbs 17:22 tells us, "A merry heart does us good, like medicine. But a broken spirit dries up bones."

If you get downsized from the company where you have worked hard for ten, twenty, even thirty years, you are ready to respond with, "All of my help comes from the Lord. Unemployment will not defeat me!" If your husband of twenty years files for divorce, you know in your heart that "No weapon formed against me will prosper," and you proceed to make the necessary moves to make a fresh start in your life.

When Joel Osteen's mother, Dodie Osteen, visited me, she instructed me to stir up the Word of God in my heart because I could never know when I might need it. I like to share that pearl of wisdom with the women I meet. Loving yourself means preparing yourself for the battles ahead. It is having a good defense when Satan tries to attack or offend you. Stay on the ready, constantly meditating on the Word.

For the Lord sees not as man sees:
man looks on the outward appearance,
but the Lord looks on the heart.

1 Samuel 16:7

Recognize the Source of Insecurities

Brandy was seventeen years old and slightly overweight when I met her. She believed she was fat and ugly. Her mother and other family members were helping her to keep her weight from spiraling out of control. She was eating healthy meals, exercising more, and achieving better results. But at school she was still teased for being overweight. Whenever she got into an argument, someone would call her "fat," to make her angry—and it worked. Even though she claimed the insults didn't hurt, she would cry silently in her room at night. Eventually she even attempted suicide because she felt she would never be considered attractive to anyone because she would never have a model's figure.

"I think it's unfair," she told me. "If a girl is not small like the popular girls at my school, she is automatically seen as ugly. I can't wear the cute outfits the cute girls wear, so I feel like an outcast. I know it seems petty but I would get so upset just because I couldn't wear what they could wear!"

Brandy was a senior in high school and continued to hear negative comments from her peers; but things got better when she received counseling from her youth group at church. She began expressing her talents as a visual artist and poet. "My youth pastor, my parents, other family members, and friends helped," she said. "Whenever I get depressed, I meditate on the Psalms of David, such as Psalm 23 and Psalm 139. I believe that even though I'm not the size of a supermodel, I'm still lovable and beautiful. I have to remind myself constantly that when God sees me, He sees me as one of His beautiful creations. I'll always be beautiful in His eyes."

A myriad of talk shows, sitcoms, magazines, movies, ads, and commercials scream out ideals of what makes a woman "lovely" or "lovable." Most major companies use celebrity endorsements to market their products and services. By doing so, they attempt to capitalize on the insecurities of women. Makeup companies use supermodels in their advertising campaigns to manipulate women into thinking, *"This makeup will make me look as good as she does!"*

Industry markets *image.* It attempts to define what is beautiful, trendy, and acceptable. Some women feel that if they don't conform to media-hyped images they will never be lovable or acceptable. The truth is, "popular opinions" are contrary to God's thoughts about us. We must decide to conform to God's image of us. God tells us our beauty comes from within. We can either follow the advice of today's market consultants or live by the standards set forth in the Word of God. Our decision will determine whether or not we will experience emotional wholeness or emotional turmoil.

I encourage you to post your favorite Scripture about God's love for you on your social media pages. Or, you may choose to write your own love note from God and post it. Imagine God saying, "I love you because . . ." and then reflect on that love every time you look in the mirror, until it becomes a natural instinct for you to reflect on God's love for you.

*Do not let your adorning be
external—the braiding of hair and the putting
on of gold jewelry, or the clothing you wear—
but let your adorning be the hidden person of the
heart with the imperishable beauty of a gentle
and quiet spirit, which in God's
sight is very precious.*

1 Peter 3:3–4

Be Authentic

My daughters and I went shopping in New York once. We were having a ball, going to some of the discount places. One of my daughters found a fragrance store and bought a fragrance she wanted. It had the famous name, and the familiar box. She was so delighted to find this perfume—and at a great price. But when we got home and she opened up that box, it didn't smell anything like she'd expected. In fact, it was horrible. Turns out she had gotten a cheap knockoff, and as a result she was very disappointed.

We want to avoid being like that knockoff fragrance. We want to be real about who we say we are. If you're a Christian, it's not enough for you to talk the talk; you have to walk the walk. When people come in contact with you, they should experience the genuine love of Christ, the real thing. They shouldn't encounter somebody who is mean, rude, hateful, fussy, cursing, and carrying on—being a discredit to the Kingdom of God.

Be real with yourself. Don't be kind in church, then mean and nasty on the way home. Your children are not fooled. It won't do to just act out that old nursery rhyme: *This is the way we go to church, go to church, go to church* . . . At church you're all smiles: "Praise the Lord, Brother." "How are you?" "Blessed!" Then, after church, you get in the car and you're cursing your kids out. That's not showing them that God's love is real. They begin to associate churchgoing with fakeness, and they will want no part of it. If you're fussy with your children at home, be your fussy self in church—until it becomes embarrassing enough to you to actually change your fussiness. If you're sour at home, let your church family see your sourness. They may help you grow out of it. Be the same person wherever you go.

It's okay to have a sour moment or experience a negative emotion. But don't get stuck on those bad feelings for a whole day. Jesus experienced all the human emotions we face. The Bible tells us in Hebrews 4:15, "For we do not have a high priest who is unable to empathize with our weaknesses, but we have one who has been tempted in every way, just as we are—yet he did not sin." Jesus wept. He got tired. People got on his nerves. But he knew what to do in his moments of weakness. He knew to go boldly to God for grace, for supernatural assistance.

I've heard some Christian parents justify yelling at their kids. "I'm just keeping it real," they will say. That doesn't make it right. Get real with why you're feeling overwhelmed or irritated. Ask God for help.

Romans 12:9 talks about an authentic love. It says, "Let your love be sincere." Let your love be a real thing. The word *authentic* means *to be real.* It means *to be genuine.* It means *not to be false, not to misrepresent.* Now, I'm not talking about being false through the use of superficial beauty enhancers. I'm not saying throw away your makeup, reject nail enhancements, and shun all hair extensions and weaves. Not at all. I'm talking about being sincere about who you are on the inside. Accept who you are on the inside. God accepts you—He made you! Be the same person wherever you go. Let your character be consistent. Be authentic. Be the real you. Be the best you can be.

MANY TIMES, IF WE'RE not careful, we can prevent a breakthrough from occurring in our life by having the wrong attitude. Granted, life gets hard sometimes, and some situations just plain stop us in our tracks. But we must press through painful emotions. When things don't go as planned, or when people hurt or disappoint us, it's hard to see the light at the end of the tunnel. However, during those hard times, we must delve into the Word and stay close to God more than ever.

A woman who knows her value and worth is precious. She knows she's capable, intelligent, and strong. The Bible says it's rare to find a woman who is established in that truth. A woman who embraces her value doesn't depreciate over time. She's like a fine jewel that becomes more valuable over time thanks to the joy she has given to the lives of those around her.

Get a Grip

Self-love does not mean narcissism. An inflated sense of entitlement and selfishness will lead to huge disappointments. Give yourself a reality check and be okay with who you are. Whether you are an eight-dollar-an-hour retail worker, an eighty-thousand-a-year mid-level professional, or a seven-figure sister, know that God loves you just as you are. We can't all be on television, get lucrative record deals, or marry billionaires. Billy Joel had a hit song, "Just the Way You Are." He sang, *"I love you just the way you are."* That's how God feels about each of us.

Manage your expectations and forget about perfectionism. We are all human. We make mistakes. We can strive to achieve and maintain high standards, but we need to forgive ourselves, and others, when we fall short. Like and accept who you are, be comfortable in your own skin and happy in your own company. Knowing God's view of you prepares you to accept and love others and to love in a way that brings joy, not heartache.

Grace be to you, and peace,
from God our Father, and from the
Lord Jesus Christ. Blessed be the God
and Father of our Lord Jesus Christ,
who has blessed us with all spiritual
blessings in heavenly places in Christ.

EPHESIANS 1:2–3

Speak Blessings Over Your Life

Ephesians 1:2 tells us, "Grace and peace be multiplied unto you through the knowledge of God, and of Jesus our Lord. According as his divine power hath given unto us all things that [pertain] unto life and godliness." It's up to us to get the knowledge of God and Jesus Christ so that we may experience the peace and grace that God has available for us. We may be struggling with guilt, for instance. Many people struggle with the guilt of something they did in a moment of indiscretion. When we understand that God is a loving and forgiving God, we don't have to struggle with that guilt anymore. We can face whatever the consequences are, forgive ourselves, and go on to enjoy the blessings God guides us to.

You are blessed now. Your family is blessed, your children are blessed, your marriage is blessed. We don't have to struggle to get blessed. The Bible tells us we are already blessed. But we have to get this message down in our Spirit, and that's where we have to stand.

We read Ephesians 1:2–3, which says we are blessed, but we believe the lies of our circumstances more than we believe the Word of God. We look at our circumstances and think, "I'm not blessed. Look at all this debt I've got"; or "Blessed? My child is out of control. My spouse is running around, cheating on me, and you say I'm blessed?"

Yes. We are blessed regardless of our circumstances. When we believe we are blessed, we are not relying on our senses or circumstances. The Word of God says Satan will continue to defeat us with circumstances and through conversations with us that will cause us to question God's Word. To experience the promise of God's blessing in our lives, we've got to stand on something stronger than our feelings and believe something more solid than what we discern with our human senses.

We've got to tap into what's beyond this natural realm. We've got to trust God and what He says.

To experience God's love in our life, we've got to know that we already are blessed. That's not based on how anyone treats us, and that's not based on the material possessions we receive. That's based on what God promises. Remind yourself daily, and affirm it aloud: "I am already blessed. My work is already blessed. My relationships are already blessed. My past is already blessed. My future is already blessed. By the grace of God, I am blessed."

Exercises

OPENING PRAYER

Father God, I come to you with an open heart, standing ready for Your preparation. Father God, I know that now is the time. I thank You for bringing me to the lessons and exercises You provide here so that I can more fully experience love.

1. **EMBRACE YOUR FEMININITY**

A woman's value shows in how she takes care of herself. It's okay to look great and enhance your femininity—even in challenging times—by keeping proper grooming and hygiene, by keeping your hair styled, nails and teeth clean, and adding a nice aroma to your skin. Remember, you are an awesome, unique creation, so adorn yourself as such. When you allow yourself to look and feel your best, you will be less likely to compare yourself to other women. Here are a few tips to help you enhance your femininity and draw positive attention to yourself:

* Wear clothing that enhances your figure, such as a tailored blazer, an A-line skirt, or a conservatively cut V-neck sweater. Stay away from clothes that are too tight or revealing.
* Apply makeup with a light hand in natural or bright light so you don't overdo it. It may be best to initially allow a professional to help you if you are not sure how to apply makeup properly.
* Be modest when using perfume; be sure not to use too much.
* Allow a man to open doors for you, pull out your chair at a restaurant, or help you with your coat.

2. ## MAINTAIN YOUR HEALTH

After giving birth to my three daughters, I made
a conscious decision to always take care of myself.
That's why I eat properly and exercise regularly. By
loving and taking care of our physical bodies, we
can show love to others. We can't give them our best
when we don't look and feel our best. Many women
struggle with health challenges such as high blood
pressure, heart problems, diabetes, and many other
ailments due to unhealthy habits. It's important that
we eat the healthy foods we need, which includes
vegetables, fruits, and the necessary supplements.
We also need plenty of water, sunshine, and exercise.
And plenty of rest. It's important, as well, that
we discover how we can rid ourselves of stress.
Recognize what causes you stress and take steps to
reduce the stress.

3. ## INVEST IN YOURSELF

I want to encourage you to invest in yourself. Do
something that makes you feel good about you!
Go to a spa. Take a day off. Get a new hairstyle.
Get a manicure and/or pedicure. Try a new and
challenging sport. Take a class. Volunteer in an
organization where you can express your talents
and feel the rewards of sharing those talents.

Journal Questions/Prompts

WHAT MAKES YOU VALUABLE?

What makes something valuable? The sacrifice it took to produce it, the price it costs, the effort it takes to obtain it, and the unique talents involved.

1. **THE SACRIFICE**—Write a thank-you note to a parent or guardian—whether or not they are still alive to show appreciation. *Thank them for the sacrifices they made for you. Did they instill pearls of wisdom, buy your clothes and food throughout your childhood instead of spending all their hard-earned money on themselves? Thank them for it. Did they take time to attend your games or plays at school? Did they take time to talk to you and teach you important life lessons? Appreciate the sacrifices made for you that helped you to become who you are.*

2. **THE PRICE**—The value of a certain thing is determined by how much it costs. Have you considered the price of your education? Even if you went to public school, taxpayers paid for you to attend school for at least twelve years! Consider what you have that you treasure most. Look around in your home. Consider

the cost of your belongings—not just the price tag. Which mentors, friends, or family members have invested in you or helped you see value in your life? Their time and labor was a valuable gift to you. Consider value others have given you, which you may have overlooked. Recognize that this value is part of who you have become. *Write down reminders of the value you have received.*

3. THE EFFORT—Reflect on the effort it took to bring you into this world. Do you know how long your mother was in labor to have you? Have you considered the emotional energy expended to raise and discipline you? Have you considered efforts others have extended on your behalf? *Think about it and write down the efforts that come to mind.*

4. THE UNIQUENESS—What special gifts, talents, passions, ideas, or qualities do you have? Do you have a passion or knack for doing something well (for example, getting along well with people and bringing people together)? Do you have a talent (for example, singing, or making jewelry)? Do you have a personality uniquely suited for success in sales? Consider what is special about you. *In your journal write about when you discovered this unique quality in yourself and how it has blossomed since then. Imagine how this treasure will become even more valuable in the future.*

Initial Thoughts

Breakthrough

Growth

More Growth

Practice of New Understanding

Mastery of New Understanding

PART III

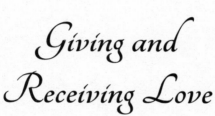

Giving and Receiving Love

Love never gives up, never loses faith, is always hopeful, and endures through every circumstance.

1 CORINTHIANS 13:7

FINDING LOVE

I WAS IMMEDIATELY ATTRACTED TO CREFLO THE first time I laid eyes on him. I loved everything about him—his strength, his command, and his conviction in the Lord. He was handsome, too! I told my friend I wanted to marry him, or someone just like him. Now, after twenty-seven years of marriage, I can honestly say, "I still deeply love this man!" I love his resilience. I love his loyal commitment to God, to me, to our family. I adore his commitment to health and long life. I love the life we've built together. I thank God for him daily.

Creflo and I became friends in the Bible study group that he led on the campus where we both were enrolled. He had a girlfriend when we first met, and there were a couple of guys on campus asking me out. But the only way they could date me was to join me for Bible study, because that's where my heart was—with the Lord.

I would wear bright clothes, colorful sundresses and sandals, knowing I would run into Creflo on our way to class or see him in Bible study. We were good friends for a year before we started dating. Neither one of us had money at the time, so our dates were limited—tennis, breakfast, or a dollar movie. The first time Creflo mentioned marriage, it was not a down-on-one-knee proposal. He mentioned in passing that we should marry. I told him we could not get married as long as he was living in his mother's house. Also, I was determined to finish college before I got married. My mother had always insisted that I complete college in order to be able to take care of myself.

Creflo and I dated for about two years, and got married two weeks after my college graduation. We moved into an apartment in Riverdale, Georgia, ten minutes from the airport. I worked at a Federal Express call center, and he worked as an educational therapist at a mental health hospital. We lived a very thrifty lifestyle. We kept to a budget of thirty dollars per week for entertainment, and so we would rent movies instead of going out to the theater. We were determined to save money, determined to see God's manifestation of financial prosperity.

We were young and in love, but as a married couple, neither one of us knew what it would take to have a successful marriage. We both had issues rooted in our upbringing. The men in his family had a history of womanizing. For my part, I had seen my mother suffer heartbreaks from my father, and I was determined I would never be vulnerable to a man the way she was. Creflo had also recently begun raising a teen-age boy named Greg. When I became a wife, I also became an instant mother to a freshman in high school. I didn't know how to be a wife, let alone a mother to a teenage son. I prayed and read the Bible a great deal, but, looking back, a lot was going on.

That first year of marriage was quite an adjustment. Six months after our wedding, we were blessed to move into our first house, a starter home, which the wife of Creflo's former pastor—she was also a real estate agent—helped us find. We had started our own church. We were in church Sundays, Wednesday evenings, and Saturday mornings for prayer ser-vices. Our church was very small—probably twenty-five members—and we had to be involved in every aspect. We made time for each other, of course, but building our church was the priority.

As our ministry grew and our family grew, so did our challenges. We moved into bigger houses and bought furniture—and a lifestyle—that created a huge debt, and financial issues.

I think the success of our marriage is the result of our

being friends, and of our willingness to change and be adaptable to God's Word. It's also the result of reminding ourselves—and each other—what the Bible has to say about our roles and responsibilities. Over time, I realized I'm not perfect. I had to be quick to forgive, quick to apologize. I had to ask the Holy Spirit how I could be accommodating to my husband the way God wants me to be accommodating. I had to learn that just as there are different phases and changes in life, so it is in marriage. I think as long as Creflo and I continue to be flexible and open to change, and keep the Bible as the final authority in our home, we can continue to enjoy a successful marriage. I not only read the Bible for guidance, I ask the Holy Spirit to guide me, to guide us on what we need to do in order to meet each other's needs. The Holy Spirit may guide us, for instance, to surrender a need to control or to release certain fears.

I'm continually amazed by Creflo's desire and zeal, his willingness to get out there and obey God. I believe now, with more conviction than ever, that good relationships have everything to do with two people's wills yielding to God's will. I think the success of any relationship is going to be based on the bendability, the flexibility, the yielding of each person. We have to be able to work together, and do what needs to be done, and offset one another, and pray for one another.

$\mathcal{L}ove$ $\mathcal{P}erseveres$

I recently read an article about the oldest married couple in America. John and Ann Betar of Fairfield, Connecticut, were married on November 25, 1932. John was twenty-one when they wed, Ann was seventeen. Both were born in Syria and raised in the United States. Ann had been "arranged" to marry another man, twenty years older than she, by her parents, who believed the older man could take better care of her. But Ann was in love with John, and the pair eloped in order to be together. John became a very successful businessman, owning a popular grocery store, Betar's Market, in Bridgeport, along with other real estate investments.

According to news reports that celebrated their eighty-first anniversary on November 25, 2013, the couple had five children, fourteen grandchildren, and sixteen great-grandchildren.

Ann was a stay-at-home mother, for which her husband commended her. "She raised five children and she was a wonderful caretaker," he told reporters. The toughest challenges they faced were the deaths of two of their children, from cancer. Both children were adults when they died, but, as the couple told reporters, "No matter how many children you have or how old they are, it's the worst thing that can happen to a parent." In their golden years, they enjoy being surrounded by loving, doting grandchildren and great-grandchildren.

What is the secret to their long-lasting marriage? "We live one day at a time," John told reporters. "The family keeps us alive." He also said, "Don't hold a grudge. Forgive each other," to which Ann added, "It is unconditional love and understanding. We have had that. We consider it a blessing."

The Betars exemplify what the Bible tells us: "Love never gives up, never loses faith, and is always hopeful." Every couple gets tested, but the couples that prevail do so because of their faith and determination. We get tested with illness, death, and changes in our financial fortunes. We get tested by temptations and external influences. But when we persevere, we can experience God's love in greater measure. What began as infatuation and romance becomes deeper commitment, with more determination and the joy you both feel from having triumphed over your challenges.

Let the Grace of God Carry You

My father had a rich uncle who died and left him money. My mother said the money changed their relationship. There are different things that can change a relationship. Life causes all kinds of circumstances and opportunities to become frustrating. But it's how we deal with whatever happens that will determine whether or not we stay together. Unfortunately, after forty-nine years of marriage my parents divorced. Shortly after that my mother went home to be with the Lord. Many relationships end not because of a lack of love, but because of a lack of grace. Grace helps you become adaptable to the ins and outs, the ups and downs of life.

I think if my mother had learned more about God's grace, it would have made all the difference for her. When we believe in God's grace, no surprise or tragedy is going to totally ruin our life. We seek God and ask Him what to do with our families, with our children, and how to help them through their teenage years. When we have grace, we adjust to all the ins and outs that life brings our way.

Creflo and I have made it to our twenty-seventh anniversary by the grace of God. There were some challenges that we had to overcome. Although I knew from the beginning that it was God's will for Creflo to teach and minister, I did not know it would mean me being left alone many nights, caring for our children sometimes feeling like a single parent. I had some attitude adjusting to do. I had to decide whether or not I was willing to adjust to his calling. "Okay, God," I said, "I dedicate my husband to You. He's Yours first and mine second. I accept that"—but it took a year or so for me to truly deal with my feelings and make the adjustments.

Sometimes we have to deal with our emotions and pray

for patience. We have to avoid being in a hurry to change our circumstances. Wait on the Lord. I thank God we were able to make it through the different changes in our lives. I am so thankful and so blessed today.

I believe that if we stay with God and stay in faith, He is able to bring us out of any unfavorable situation. My spiritual mother, Gloria Copeland, would tell me, "Taffi, marriage just gets better and better." She was right. It's so good to be around people who are full of faith and full of the Word.

It is good for a man not to have sexual relations with a woman. But since sexual immorality is occurring, each man should have sexual relations with his own wife, and each woman with her own husband. The husband should fulfill his marital duty to his wife, and likewise the wife to her husband.

1 CORINTHIANS 7:1–3

Find One Hundred Ways

I recently heard about a young woman who was learning to do just that in her marriage.

The young woman said her aunt's advice on marriage was simple at first. "Just give him some," Aunt Rose had advised. "Never deny your husband. I don't care if you're mad at him or not. Just turn over and give him some. Give him some when he wants some, and give him some when he doesn't." Aunt Rose has been married more than forty years and was falling in love with her husband all over again in their retirement. The younger woman was at a point in her marriage where she could not imagine growing old with her husband. Things had gotten bad between them. They didn't communicate anymore. Their marriage had become one of those "sexless marriages" she'd read about.

"What about when he doesn't want your loving anymore?" the young woman asked her Aunt Rose. The young woman felt rejected by her husband. Aunt Rose suggested that she not take her husband's emotional and sexual withdrawal personally. "There are plenty of ways to love a man," Aunt Rose said. "Take note of what he likes, what's special to him, and love him through that. Take time to polish all his shoes one day. Set them up nicely where he will notice the shine. Fold the laundry that he's left in the laundry basket all week. There's plenty of ways to love a man. I told one young woman, if your husband's a vegetarian, then you love him through the best vegetarian meals you can cook! There are plenty of ways to love a man. Sex is only one way."

The young woman considered her husband's love for food. When they were dating, he took her to all the finest restaurants in their city. They often watched the Food Channel together when times were good. They shopped for cookbooks together. She served him breakfast in bed, and he enjoyed it. But as he began to withdraw from her, for reasons she could not understand, he claimed that her meals upset his stomach. Heartbroken, she confessed to her aunt that nothing she tried seemed to work. Her aunt offered another pearl of wisdom.

"All couples go through some things," Aunt Rose explained. "You do what you can do and don't worry about the rest. You can still stir up a good meal so you're delighting his senses. He's gon' smell it even if he doesn't eat," she said. "You don't need his permission or cooperation to fill your home with delicious aromas. That's standing on faith. You've got to know that despite whatever your husband is going through, the God spirit within him will appreciate your love offering. Ask God to guide you in your love offerings, and trust that God will."

When times get tough, we've got to stand on God's promises and walk in faith. Even when a husband is physically absent—off on a business trip or emotionally disconnected, hibernating in his man cave—we can offer a loving gesture, a heartfelt prayer. We can send him a note of thanks to help sustain God's love in our marriage.

First Corinthians 13 tells us how God defines love: "Love suffers long, and is kind." That's an instruction to be patient. You have determined to experience God's love in your marriage. So when your husband has been promising to fix the bathroom door for six months, or promising to take you on a date for a year, you know better than to nag or give him a nasty attitude every chance you get. Instead, you respond with kindness, appreciating the other good deeds your husband does—going to work, going to church, spending time with the children, keeping up his health, paying bills, tending to his aging parents, helping mentor nieces and nephews. Because you love him, you find reasons to be kind to him.

The Bible tells us, "Love envies not." If we're not careful, we can envy our husband's relationship with the children when he seems closer to them or more welcomed by them than we are. We may find ourselves envying his success, if we do not keep our mind on loving him God's way.

The Bible tells us love is not puffed up. We can't hold ourselves higher because we think we're more spiritual than he is. Maybe we go to church more, or serve in more ministries in the church, and then we believe we're on a higher spiritual plane. No. God tells us that love is not puffed up. If we want to experience God's love in our marriage, we can't be puffed up.

The Bible says, "Love does not behave rudely, seeks not her own, is not easily provoked." So, no, you cannot justify going to his job, acting the fool because you had an argument—or, worse, because he didn't come home when he was supposed to last night. Some things we're going to take to God in prayer. We're not going to seek retribution. Forget about *He stressed me out at home last night, so you know what? I'm gonna go to his job and stress him out.* No. To experience God's love in our marriage, we're going to do what God tells us to do, and let God handle the rest.

The Bible tells us love bears all things, believes all things, hopes all things, endures all things. That means that even when the marriage looks grim—when your husband is not romantic with you, and hasn't been for some time, and you haven't taken a vacation together in years, and communication between you is stifled—you still believe in your love, because God told you love believes all things.

Love does not dishonor. In other words, even when we are rightfully angry, we are not calling his mother to tell her how rotten her son is behaving. We are not calling his sisters and his best friend, telling them all our problems, because we are believing God will solve the problems and clear them away like yesterday's clouds.

When we ask God to show us how to embrace His love in our marriage, He will direct us in unique ways to express His love in our unique union. Sometimes God calls for us to love our husband differently from the way we saw our grandmothers love their husbands, and differently from how our mothers loved theirs. We have to seek God's guidance on embracing His love in our marriage. When my mother filed for divorce after forty-nine years of marriage, I felt sad, but also worried. Could that possibly happen to me? Was divorce genetic? Would problems that had persisted in my marriage leave one of us to file for divorce just when we should be settling into our glorious golden years? Immediately I dispelled the thought of divorce.

Sometimes when the going gets rough I have to remember what I loved about my husband in the beginning.

Healing from Rejection and Other Painful Emotions

Before we can get to the *glory* years of marriage, we must persevere through the *gory* years of marriage. The emotional junk we unwittingly bring into our marriages will guarantee us some gory years.

When we feel deeply in love, especially when we are dating, or in the honeymoon phase of our marriage, many of our painful emotions seem to have disappeared. That "in love" feeling is like balm in Gilead. When we're in love, we feel like Lauryn Hill in that song "Nothing Even Matters." Being in love makes us feel brand-new. We have met our mate, and his love affirms us in ways we never imagined. We are so excited about hearing from him, seeing him, being with him every day, nothing else matters. Whatever negative emotions we were feeling before he came gallivanting into our life seem to have vanished with the wind. We feel better than we ever felt before. We forget about all those negative emotions—until they come back to the surface for us to finally resolve them.

Marriage will not erase all those negative emotions. In fact, marriage may be the vehicle through which you finally are delivered. In marriage we are forced to deal with those negative emotions and to seek healing. If we had issues of fear, abandonment, and/or rejection before we fell in love, those issues will come up again in our marriage. Those issues may even be compounded by marriage, because now we've got someone up close and personal witnessing what we are dealing with and calling us to account for it.

Early in my marriage, I sometimes felt neglected, believing Creflo was spending too much of his time in the ministry. I would often become upset with Creflo because I didn't feel that I was as important to him as I should have been. I didn't understand why he was so ambitious about developing the ministry and so forth. During my first pregnancy, and right before delivery, he was traveling all around the world, a time when I thought he should have been at home with me, holding my hand. He wasn't intentionally being insensitive and distant toward me, but I saw it that way because we allowed the ministry to be our world instead of God and family.

As time passed, I eventually became so frustrated that I had to look to God instead of my husband for my happiness. And as I began to focus on God, I realized my husband was simply trying to do what God had called him to do. It wasn't long before my husband started looking better to me! I was no longer angry with him. It's amazing how a situation can remain the same but our experience in it can change drastically—because we perceive it differently.

Every woman wants to be accepted and feel important. As the mother of three daughters and two sons, I've come to understand this even more. In fact, whatever stage of life we are in, no matter how old we are, we always want to know we are accepted—no matter what. When we feel rejected on some level, it can produce feelings of inferiority, anger, and self-doubt.

The world today is full of hurting, rejected women who really want to be loved. Roots of rejection can go down deep, causing a host of emotional challenges and behavior that can surface later in life. In fact, many adults are actually rejected children on the inside, doing everything in their power to gain validation through someone or something outside of God. They seek relationships, jobs, and material goods to compensate for what is missing inside. The negative emotion of rejection continues to fuel their insecurities and low self-esteem.

When a woman does not deal with the feelings of rejection in her soul, she becomes open to being taken advantage of. Because of her need to be accepted, she may compromise her standards or values in an attempt to secure a relationship. Doing this only leads to more problems and eventually ends up costing her peace of mind, emotional well-being, and, in some cases, her life itself.

In order to deal with the pain of rejection and other painful emotions, we must have the courage to ask God, and to look within. If we deny having deeper issues, we delay our deliverance. Looking within may require us to face some very tough issues, but as we expose and uncover them, we allow God to do His work in us. Then the experience becomes a testimony to others of the goodness and faithfulness of God.

Recognize the Root of Your Problems Hint: It's Not Your Husband

Kate, a young woman I met through ministry who grew up feeling unwanted, has reached a place in her spiritual walk where she is content with what God is doing in her life. She believes God has healed her from the pain of rejection and the bitterness that was causing her to sabotage herself through addictions and unhealthy relationships. She said she had so much bitterness and hatred at one time in her life that she didn't care about anyone or anything, because she believed no one cared about her.

Her first marriage was emotionally painful; her first husband had an affair, and there were other problems in the marriage, as well. At the time, she didn't realize that her deeper issues were leading her into disastrous relationships and situations. "In my first marriage I didn't even know how to relate to men because I never had an example of what a good marriage looks like," she said. "I didn't respect men because I saw that my mother didn't respect men. They were just to be used for whatever you needed. I never saw any value in them whatsoever beyond that."

But when she began seeking answers from God, He revealed to her the root of her problem.

"The Lord showed me how my sister and I were orphaned in our mother's womb," she said. "My mother became pregnant with us as a result of an affair with another man. Her husband left her, and then our father, whom she had the affair with, left her. He didn't want to have anything to do with us. At that point, my mother began to shut down emotionally, and soon she didn't want to have anything to do with us, either."

Kate and her twin sister grew up in a household where there was no parental love or nurturing. They both experienced emotional turmoil as a result, and began to make unwise decisions, especially in the area of relationships. Kate said she would often sabotage her relationships or cut the relationship off at the first sign of trouble, fearing that rejection and abandonment were right around the corner.

Kate is remarried now and has a son from her previous marriage. She is grateful that God allowed her to find a good man. She is hopeful that this marriage will be better, since she has rooted out some of her own issues that in the past might have sabotaged it.

Rejection is a painful emotion that severely impacts our self-esteem. It can move us to do things we would never do under ordinary circumstances. It can cause us to make decisions that are not in our best interest. When we do not allow God to be our primary source of acceptance and love, we can easily feel rejected by others.

Many women struggle with rejection, especially where personal relationships are concerned. Women, designed, as we are, to nurture babies in our womb, are innately interested in relationships. Men, on the other hand, are built and socialized for hunting, conquering to survive. Because women are wired to be relational, the pain we feel when we are rejected by a loved one can be intense, even unbearable.

Often, unhealed wounds from the past produce a rejection consciousness, creating a vicious cycle. Because an old boyfriend stopped returning your calls two weeks before he broke up with you, the first time your husband fails or neglects to return a call you panic. You fear he is setting you up for a breakup. You don't consider that he may be legitimately busy, or simply needs some time alone. That's a rejection consciousness at work. You must pray to break the cycle. Change your consciousness from expecting rejection to expecting acceptance.

Rejection is a particularly dangerous emotion because there are so many other emotions tied to it. For example, if rejection is taking up residence in your heart, it won't be long before depression comes on the scene. And depression, which is anger turned inward, will take you to a place of darkness, despair, and hopelessness. These feelings are designed to move you away from the plan God has for your life. And these feelings can wreak havoc on your marriage.

So how can we overcome rejection consciousness? By being mindful of the fact that everything about us, from the way our bodies are shaped to the personality that makes us unique, was fashioned by our loving Creator. We should focus on our beauty, individuality, and special gifts every day. God never rejects us. God accepts us just as we are!

*A virtuous and worthy wife
[earnest and strong in character]
is a crowning joy to her husband,
but she who makes him ashamed
is as rottenness in his bones.*

PROVERBS 12:4, AMP.

Why Do We Do What We Do?

Sometimes we carry a great deal of baggage into a relationship instead of getting free first. At the beginning of my marriage, I had a hard time dealing with the fact that I was supposed to submit to my husband as the head of our household. As a young child, I saw my mother endure things that I was not willing to let any man take me through. My mother thought that my father was philandering and disrespectful. As a result, every time Creflo tried to help me by giving me suggestions or asking me to do things, I instantly rebelled. I felt he was trying to control me and belittle me. Over time, I came to realize that I was blessed with a good husband, and that I should not make him suffer for the wrongs of others. Asking for God's help and studying God's Word in this area freed me.

On the other hand, Creflo had to recognize when his insecurities were causing him to be overbearing. It took him years to realize he wasn't the only wise one in the house. I had to constantly remind him that he was blessed to have me, too! We both had to learn about each other and grow. Being free of our baggage allows us to become more compassionate and to see things from the perspective of others, even when their perspective is wrong.

Most people who act out of unloving motives do so

because of their unresolved issues. We must pray for each other with a sincere heart, realizing that the same God who freed you is able to free them, too.

Wedded bliss will allow us an escape from dealing with our negative emotions, but only for a while. We can fill our days with busyness, but at some point we will have to take time to recognize, understand, appreciate, and be who we really are. We may try to blame our husband for making us feel bad. But when we are centered in God, putting God first, we understand that our husband is not the problem.

There are often strongholds that are difficult to overcome on our own. They sometimes require months, or even years, of counseling before healing can begin. When we have experienced rejection, abandonment, depression, fear, or other painful emotions that we can't seem to overcome on our own, we should seek reliable professional help. It's okay to ask others for help. God often sends other people to help us through trials. In fact, admitting that we have a problem or need help is the first step toward recovery. There are great counselors out there who can help us work through our difficulties.

We can talk to a trustworthy Christian counselor, minister, or friend about our past sins, hurts, and struggles, and ask for prayer. We should first follow the Holy Spirit's lead when choosing someone who will agree with us. The Bible tells us, in James 5:16, "Confess your sins to each other and pray for each other so that you may be healed. The earnest prayer of a righteous person has great power and produces wonderful results."

After nearly three decades, I strongly believe in the bond of marriage. I believe marriage works. It can work. It does work. It is working, but there are tools and there are keys that can help. It doesn't just happen by chance because, as we know, homes and families are breaking up every single day. We can begin to get a hold of the right tools, the right skills, and the right keys to manage and mature our marriage. Ultimately, it is God who sustains our marriage. But, like going to school to get an education, or learning new skills at our job in order to perform the tasks required, we must do our part.

Whenever we are having issues in our relationships, especially in marriage, we need to get quiet so that we can receive guidance from the Holy Spirit. We have to be sure we take the time to clear our minds and pray so that we can hear Him. At times, we may need help. It is okay to seek counsel from mature fellow Christians when relationship issues grow out of control. It is perfectly fine to seek professional counseling, particularly from a counselor who respects our religious beliefs and can support us in them. But the Holy Spirit should be our ultimate guide. He will always lead us to make the right choices.

The following are some tips to help you experience God's love in your marriage:

Fortify Your Marriage

I met the late Coretta Scott King once, very briefly, but studying her life has ministered to me a great deal. I met her at a gala held in her honor in Atlanta many years ago. Although our encounter was short, it was very encouraging. I admired her temperament. She was calm and captivating. I just thought she was an incredible person. The gala was a black tie affair, and when I was getting dressed that evening, my husband had commented on the coat I chose to wear. It was a fuchsia cashmere coat, trimmed in fuchsia fur, and Creflo said, "I *know* you're not wearing that loud thing!" Well, I did, and as soon as we walked into the reception hall, I felt like all eyes were on me. I felt so out of place. But I was excited about honoring Mrs. King because I had read all of her books and studied her life. I had read about her activism before she even married Martin. I had read about how their house was bombed—twice. I read how she had been prepared for that role because, while growing up, her father's business was burned to the ground, allegedly by racists, and their house was burned down, too. Her life was dramatic and amazing, and I was thrilled to be at an event honoring her.

Okay, so I'm standing there, embarrassed about my coat, but excited about the moment, and then she walks in. We all formed a welcoming line, and she began shaking each person's hand as she moved down the line. When she got to me, as she held my hand, she smiled and said, "I like your coat!" That encounter inspired me for many years. It was a nod of acknowledgment, of confidence in my tastes, my likes, and my decisions. It confirmed for me that it's okay to be different and to stand out.

I get strength also from reading the stories of the women in the Bible. I love Judge Deborah in the Bible, because she held her own. God used her to deliver the people of Israel from the brutal rule of a foreign king. She was a prophetess and trusted the instruction she heard from God. The story of Ruth and Naomi also can minister to us about honor. Naomi and her daughter-in-law exemplify honorable love and loyalty. After they both lost their husbands, their friendship sustained them.

Thirty years ago, I contacted Dr. Betty Price, wife of Apostle Fred Price, founder of the Crenshaw Christian Center in Los Angeles. Even before I was married, and later, as our church grew, I reached out to her and asked about being a pastor's wife. I thought she had good experience and could give me guidance on what to do and what not to do. I needed to know about becoming a role model for women in church. Since I had not grown up in a church, I didn't know much about church folk. I didn't know what to make of their expectations. Creflo was focused on teaching God's word, and I wanted to know how to support him.

She relieved me of a lot of pressure. One of the most

challenging aspects of being a pastor's wife is managing others' expectations. People expect you to behave as they think you, as a Christian leader, should. People have certain expectations of what women should and should not do. I had to learn not to measure myself by, or be bound to, other people's expectations of me and my role at the church, or by their expectations of my children and husband. Dr. Price helped me understand that.

I still call her for advice. She's a very wise woman. Dr. Betty and Apostle Price were married in March of 1953, and their marriage is still going strong sixty years later! She has advised me on my marriage, raising my kids, managing my home, and on church business. She wasn't as involved in the business side of their church as I was, because she stayed home to raise their four children. She advised that Creflo and I pray for guidance. I now see that we should not have spent so much time traveling, away from our kids. I was out on the road a lot with Creflo, and I think our kids were deeply affected by that. We bore the brunt of it as they got into their teens.

At World Changers Church International, we have a very active marriage ministry. We host monthly events for couples, such as workshops that focus on romance, intimacy, communication, and finances. We watch movies and have extensive conversations about them. We enjoy skits and role-playing. We learn from each other.

I have heard lots of testimony from couples who were

on the brink of divorce when they joined our marriage ministry. They say their marriage was supernaturally saved. They could see the benefit from the very practical exercises they followed, as well as through fellowshipping with other couples. But I believe that because they invited God to be more present in their marriage, and they took steps to do all they could, God moved miraculously and turned their marriages around. There's one couple who've been married at least sixty years—their mere presence is an inspiration to us all. Another couple who've been married forty years have shared with us their testimony of surviving heartbreak and drug addiction and loss of trust. They were separated at one time, about to divorce, but God reunited them. God led them both to church, called the husband, redeemed from addiction, into ministry, and they raised their family in a Christian home.

Marriage is serious business, and I believe that just as we are wise to seek mentors in our professional lives, we should wisely seek mentors for our married lives. Whether we find marriage mentors in church, in our family, or on our jobs, marriage mentors can help fortify us for the long haul. They can encourage us when things get tough. They are the ones who will tell us, "Hold on! Change is coming."

I encourage couples to fortify their marriage with prayer and thanksgiving; through studying the Word, meditating on the Word, and through finding a good marriage mentor or ministry.

Submit

The Bible tells us, in Ephesians 5:22, "Wives, submit yourselves to your husbands, as is fitting in the Lord." We have
to be real in our marriages when it comes to submission. It's
a challenge for many of us. I read that Coretta Scott King
had that part of their wedding vows removed. She wouldn't
say it! But I also read of many instances when she did
yield to her husband. He had advised her not to attend his
first March on Washington because she was pregnant and
he was not sure what to expect on the trip. She wanted to
join him for that march, but yielded to his authority. She
also did not want to name their son Martin Luther King
III, because she considered it too much pressure to name a
child after such an accomplished parent. But here, too, she
yielded to him.

Submission has been a real challenge for me. Early in
our marriage, there were times when I submitted blindly,
and times when I refused to submit at all, determined not
to be taken advantage of. I had to learn when to hold and
when to fold. Sometimes we need to hold the line on something. And sometimes we need to go along with our husband's plan. Submission doesn't mean saying yes all the
time. No man needs a wife saying yes all the time. Sometimes, as a wife, you've got to be the voice of reason. I
believe if we read what God tells us about submission, and

pray for the Holy Spirit to guide us, we can find our perfect balance in submission.

Build a Grace-Based Relationship

It took me a while to realize that some of the things that my husband says I'm just not going to understand. He can say something, and my response is, "What? Where'd you get *that* from? Who taught you that? What book have you been reading?" But I had to learn that that's just how he is. That's his thinking. It's just out of the box. I should have known that from the beginning, right? I had to learn that our marriage was not based on total agreement every day of our lives for the rest of our lives. I had to learn that our marriage would be sustained not by my efforts to understand—or to please, or to do anything. Our marriage could only be sustained by the grace of God. We've learned how to agreeably disagree.

The Bible tells us, in Ephesians 2:8–9, "For by grace you have been saved through faith; and that not of yourselves, it is the gift of God; not as a result of works, that no one should boast."

God's acceptance of us is not based on what we do. In the days of the Old Testament, people believed they had to earn God's grace. They believed the people in their life had to earn their favor as well. If you had a big nose you weren't accepted. If you had a bunion on your foot you weren't accepted. If you had some kind of deformity you weren't accepted, according to the law and customs of the land. That was just how it was. It was hard. I know I couldn't have made it then. If you had any mark or blemish, you were condemned. Even the lamb had to be without blemish. It had to be perfect. It had to be flawless in order to be accepted as a sacrifice. But God enlightened us.

God doesn't hold conditions over us. He says that He's accepted us as we are in Jesus. We, in our marriage, should be the same way. We should be willing to accept one another, receive one another, without a lot of qualifications and conditions. If you're saying, "I love him as long as he's paying these bills," that's conditional love. You should love him even if God blessed *you* with the income to pay all the bills. You may be saying, "I love him as long as he can get my hair fixed and my nails done every week." Yes indeed, I've heard it: "I will love him as long as he [you name it]." Conditional love places all these hurdles for someone to jump in order to merit your love. That's not how God sees us. Conditional love is fear-based love.

We set up conditions and require someone to prove their love over and over again when we are afraid that if we don't keep them jumping through hoops they may leave us. God's love for us is not based on fear. It's based on grace. God's love for us is not based on anything that we have done. It's based on everything that Jesus has done.

A grace-based relationship is based on the righteousness of God, and on our agreement to be right with God. Grace-based relationships compel us to forgive, just as God forgives, and to love as God loves—unconditionally.

Avoid Shame and Blame

The Bible tells us, in 1 John 1:9, "If we confess our sins, he is faithful and just to forgive us our sins and to cleanse us from all unrighteousness."

God doesn't hold our sins against us, and we shouldn't hold our husband's sins against him. Let it go! God wants us to live without shame and without blame. We can extend that manner of love to our mate. Blame is like a curse. Constantly reminding someone of their faults or past transgressions ties them to that behavior. You are begging for them to repeat it. Each time you remind them, you are telling them you expect them to repeat it. That's not the way God works. God reminds us of our future. God tells us that our future is bright, that we have many things to look forward to. God says we should be without blame before Him in love. If our relationships are full of blame and shame, that's not God, and that's not God's best for us.

Talk show host Wendy Williams told *Essence* magazine

about how she forgave her husband after he cheated. In the June 2013 issue, Williams said, "The best advice that I can give is that if you're the one who was cheated on, whether you decide to stay or leave, forgive and forget either way." Forgiveness is the only way to keep the door open for God's love in our life. We pray the Lord's Prayer, which is based on Matthew 6:14: "Forgive us our trespasses as we forgive those who trespass against us." We have to mean it and live it. Set your will to forgive each day.

Walk in love, as Christ loved us,
a fragrant offering and sacrifice to God.

EPHESIANS 5:2

Redeem One Another

God sent His son Jesus to demonstrate redemptive love. Jesus willingly extended Himself to do the right thing when somebody else wasn't doing the right thing in order to deliver humankind from sin. That's what redemptive love is. It's not always who's doing right. It's not digging in your heels, privately vowing, "I'm not going to do right until you do right. You be ugly; I'm going to be ugly, too. You ain't the only one who knows how to be ugly. I can be just as ugly." It is redemptive love that has captured our hearts, that has captured us. It is God's redemptive love that arrests us, that seizes us in the midst of wanting to do wrong, and constrains us. It is redemptive love that calls us to come and seek God and to understand more about Him. It is God's redemptive love that restrains us from wanting to continue to practice sin.

To invite God's love more fully into our marriage, we must demonstrate redemptive love. Jesus was a Redeemer. Jesus didn't know what would happen, but yet He was willing to sacrifice and willing to give all. Often in relationships that's what's needed. Someone has to be willing to be the redeemer, otherwise the relationship will end in disappointment, disconnection, and divorce.

Maintain Common Ground

It's a great blessing when we can be fully in accord with our spouse, praying the same prayers, at the same time, in the same space. I'm happy to see that in my lifetime I see more families arriving together in church, to pray together, than in some previous generations when parents sent the children to church, or Mama took the children to church while Daddy stayed home. If you're in church but your husband is not, in addition to praying that God continues to bless him, I encourage you to find other common ground with him.

Does he play golf? Then take up golf. Is he a sports fan? Enjoy the big games of the season with him. One woman I met told me about her ninety-four-year-old grandparents who did almost everything together in their more than seventy-three years of marriage. In their younger years, the couple fished together, golfed together, partied together, and worshipped together. "They went out dancing or played cards with other couples until 3:00 a.m. Sunday morning, got home in time for a few hours of sleep, woke the kids up, and went to church together," she said. "They sang in the choir together, served as deacon and deaconess together, everything. In fact, Granddad told me he didn't really like gardening. But he decided to help Grandma with her garden, and later he found that he liked the fact that they could save lots of money by growing their own vegetables."

Continually strive to establish common ground. Also, strive to create common understanding, and respect each other's different territories. If you joined a church but your husband did not, I believe it's not God's intention for you to nag him until he joins your church and worships God your way. God tells us to let our lives light the path for others to come to Christ. God may, indeed, minister to him in other ways, or in other places. Your husband may be a doctor and God may minister examples of restoring life right there in the emergency room or the operating room. Your husband may work in finance, and God ministers to him about action and accountability right there in his office while he is crunching numbers, balancing assets and liabilities. Your husband may manage a juvenile detention center and God ministers to him daily, with lessons about crime and punishment, compassion and redemption.

Avoid Temptation

I'd like to share the testimony of another young woman I met through ministry. Dana was a successful public relations specialist. She was a God-fearing woman and attended church with her husband. But she felt neglected and rejected by him, because he took no time to romance her like he used to. She became vulnerable. She found herself attracted to a man she worked with. Their relationship began innocently enough. She confessed to him her troubles at home. He showed genuine sympathy and compassion. He began calling her on her cell phone to check up on her in the evenings. She became appreciative of his attention. Affection grew between them and they ended up in an adulterous relationship.

Dana's guilt got the best of her and she ended the affair. She confessed to her husband, and he forgave her. They decided to work on their marriage by discovering what was at the root of their problems.

"We knew that with our commitment to each other and God's grace we could get past it. We also decided not to bring it up unless we were ministering to other people about how God helped us to restore our marriage," Dana said.

Don't open the door and invite Satan into your marriage. Avoid temptation by seeking God to fulfill whatever it is you think you are lacking. The Bible tells us in 1 Corinthians 7:3, "The husband should fulfill his marital duty to his wife, and likewise the wife to her husband," but when one or the other falls short of this command, God wants us to forgive and be patient. God blessed Dana and her husband to restore their marriage. We must keep in close relationship with God to avoid temptation.

Our human needs are real, they are legitimate. We want to feel loved, respected, appreciated. But when we are not careful, Satan will offer illegitimate fixes for our legitimate unmet needs. The Bible tells us "a husband should fulfill his marital duty," but when he doesn't, we are not advised to get someone else to do it. Wait on the Lord. In the meantime, we can produce "feel-good" endorphins—through rigorous exercise, for example—and we can enjoy small releases of endorphins by smiling and laughing throughout our day.

Become Your Husband's Best Friend

When Creflo and I first got to know each other, over a period of about three years, we maintained and developed a friendship. For example, we spent time with each other engaging in enjoyable activities such as playing tennis, going to football games, going to the movies, and out to breakfast. We are still best friends today, and we enjoy spending time with each other. I'm not saying we're perfect, but we choose to close the door to the enemy in our marriage by keeping our friendship strong. The enemy can be very subtle in how he comes in to destroy marriages. We need to be sure we are watching and praying, and listening to the Holy Spirit at all times.

There is a couple who is very dear to my husband and me. They are in their sixties, and many people who know them can plainly see that they are still truly each other's best friend. Mama Jane and her husband have served in ministry with us for many years. They exemplify what it means to purposely remain in love and cultivate a lifelong friendship that is fulfilling and rewarding. Mama Jane says she hasn't always been committed to the relationship; however, through God's grace, she has grown closer and closer to her husband over the years, even through trials and tribulation.

"Before I was married, I was definitely not whole or complete at all. In my family, my father was very strict. There wasn't much more we could do besides go to church," Mama Jane said, laughing. "When my husband asked me to marry him, I said yes because I was looking for a way to escape! But, honestly I did love him, because we have always been friends. We grew up together; we've known each other since high school, and we have a lot in common."

Mama Jane moved with her husband to Chicago, which was a culture shock for both of them, having been born and raised in the South. They soon learned of the reality of gang activity on the South Side of Chicago, which was one of the toughest neighborhoods in the country. Mama Jane said they would see teenagers lying in the street.

"People would just step over them. It was heartbreaking," she said. What was also heartbreaking for her was that her husband was influenced by the ways of the big city and became addicted to cocaine. "It was awful. One day I decided I couldn't take it any longer—the cold weather, the gangs, and his addiction. I left and moved back down south with my mother," she said. By then they had a son.

"I would allow my husband to see our son when he visited, but I was adamant about not seeing him myself. Literally! I would tell my son to stand on the carport with his things, and I would watch as my husband came by to pick him up. I wouldn't even dare to come near him," she said. However, one day her husband dropped by her mother's house unannounced, and then she couldn't hide from him. "He told me that he had gotten saved, and he had changed. I said, 'Yeah, *right*!' My confidence in him was really low. I didn't trust him. We had to go out on group dates. He had to really convince me and help me to trust him again. But I'll tell you the truth—it was only by the grace of God that I accepted him back into my life. I couldn't do it on my own. God helped me to fall in love with him again. He also restored our friendship—and we are still best friends today."

Mama Jane says it wasn't long after they reconciled that her husband told her that he believed God was calling him into ministry. He was later ordained as a pastor, then as a bishop. They later had another son. The couple consider themselves blessed to have had the privilege to raise both sons in a Christian household. "I believe that many couples have problems because they stop being best friends," says Mama Jane. "They stop communicating with one another and spending time with one another. My husband and I, in the forty years we have been married, have had our share of ups and downs, but we have always had our friendship to come back to. We have agreed to change when necessary and to make adjustments for each other because we were committed to our friendship and our marriage."

*Confess to one another therefore
your faults, and pray for one another,
that you may be healed. The earnest
prayer of a righteous man makes
tremendous power available.*

JAMES 5:16

Talk

Communication is vital to a healthy marriage. We should make it a point to communicate properly with one another, even if we have to reveal our own wrongdoing, faults, distrusts, or suspicions. The Bible tells us, "Confess to one another therefore your faults"—your slips, your false steps, your offenses, your sins—"and pray for one another, that you may be healed"—restored to a spiritual tone of mind and heart. "The earnest prayer"—the heartfelt and continual prayer—"of a righteous man makes tremendous power available"—which can be dynamic in its working.

Marriage counselors say poor communication between spouses is one of the main reasons many marriages end in divorce. Many people shy away from communication in order to avoid conflict or an argument. One of my spiritual mothers, Betty Price, once said that sometimes you have to rock the boat in order to have smooth sailing. That is true. Sometimes we have to deal with those tough issues before they get out of hand. Sometimes we cannot avoid conflict. We may have to wait for just the right part of the day or night to discuss our concerns, but we should make plans to address them, and sooner rather than later. Ignoring difficult issues is never the answer.

Remember, we want our communication in our relationships to be *effective*. Our goal is to resolve issues, not simply to vent. However, in order to have effective communication, we need to understand communication and how it works. Merriam-Webster's dictionary defines *communication* as "a process by which information is exchanged between individuals." The important word here is: *exchanged*. When you purchase items from a grocery store, you give money to the cashier in order to take those items home with you. That's an exchange. Both you and the cashier receive something in the transaction, and, in a sense, you've *communicated* with one another. The same principle is at work when we look at effective communication in our relationships. There must be an exchange—where each party receives and understands the information that is given by the other.

Here are a few tips to help you improve your communication:

* Choose a time when you are both relaxed.
* Approach your spouse with a warm, loving attitude.
* Avoid blaming the other person.
* Acknowledge what you may have done to contribute to the conflict.
* Be open-minded and try to see the conflict from the other person's perspective.
* Avoid using the words *never* and *always*.
* Agree to disagree.
* Commit to be patient, as ample time will allow each of you to understand the other's point of view.

Expect and Accept the Differences

God created men and women in His image, but with our own unique qualities. However, in His infinite wisdom, He created the genders differently, by design. As a result, there is a distinct difference in the way men and women process information, deal with our emotions, behave, and communicate. Despite our many differences, God's intent was, and still is, for us to complement, love, honor, and respect each other. However, unless men and women learn to effectively communicate with the opposite sex, misunderstandings will diminish our relationships.

Couples must understand that there are natural relational differences between the genders that affect their marital communication. The fact that males and females are raised differently is a major consideration. For instance, boys are raised to be macho. They are not supposed to cry or show emotion. Girls, on the other hand, are often told it's okay to cry and to show emotions. While these differences are not bad, they can cause irreparable damage to a marriage if a couple doesn't understand the responses or expressions of their spouses.

Men and women have different needs. That should not be a surprise to anyone. However, discovering what those needs are can be a challenge. The good news is that it's not as difficult as it seems. While it appears that men and women are from two different planets, God has outlined in His Word ways in which we can be sure to meet each other's needs. But both parties in this *exchange* must be willing to understand their spouse and make the necessary adjustments.

As women, we are naturally more relational. We usually have two primary concerns: family and security. We often long for connection and intimacy in our relationships. For example, a married woman's "desire" for her husband stems from her longing for an intimate friendship and relationship with him. She wants to hear his perspective on the issues she faces in life. Although it may not seem like a big deal to him, she wants to be able to discuss and share even the little things, which fosters a sense of intimacy and trust. If she senses her spouse is not making time for her, she will more than likely suspect that his affection is going elsewhere, and that will need to be addressed.

As women, we want to be heard and validated. We must be willing to communicate these things to our spouses. It doesn't hurt to remind them of our needs. For example, we can remind them that we need to share our heart with someone at the end of the day. We need someone to laugh and cry with over issues that concern us. And we don't want to feel like our issues will be a burden, taken lightly, or simply ignored.

Of course when these things are missing in our lives, we must not seek the attention of another man to meet those needs. It is our responsibility to recognize where our husbands may be failing to meet our needs and effectively communicate to them what those needs are. Likewise, our husbands should be able to tell us when their needs are not being met, and we should be willing to make the necessary sacrifices to accommodate them.

Exercises

OPENING PRAYER

Father God, I thank You for Your creation of the wonderful relationship that is marriage. I thank You for guiding me in Your ways to be successful in marriage. Father God, I know that You said that what You have brought together, let no man put asunder. Father God, I stand boldly before You today, thanking You for blessing me with a mate, and blessing me to be a blessing to my mate. Father God, I believe that however strong my marriage is at this very moment, You are guiding me to make it even stronger in You. God, I thank You for the many wonderful characteristics of my husband, and I thank You for the many wonderful experiences I already have had with him. Cleanse my heart, Father God. Whatever feelings I have toward my husband that are not from You, take them away, Father God. In Jesus' name, I pray.

1. Write a brief summary about when and how you met your husband.

2. What qualities did you find most attractive when you were dating?

3. What characteristics turned you off as you got to know him better?

4. Consider that you have the same strengths that you see in your husband. How could you tap into those strengths within you?

5. Consider that you have the same character flaws as the ones you despise in your husband. How could you acknowledge, accept, and change those character flaws within yourself?

6. Take your time—think about this for a few weeks, at least—and list one hundred ways you can love your husband better.

7. Commit to joining a marriage ministry; find a marriage mentor; fellowship with other couples.

Journal Questions

1. Have you suffered with rejection? Have you prayed about the incident? *Take your time and think about when you first felt rejected. Go as far back in your life as you can to recall the first time you felt rejected and write about those times. Compare your feelings of rejection by your husband to earlier experiences of rejection. Do you see a pattern?*

2. Recast/reimagine the experience. How could you have behaved differently? How would your different behavior have affected the outcome?

3. Imagine experiencing those same situations in the future, but with a different mindset. Now that you are more mindful of God's unconditional love, how can you be less affected by what may be someone else's intentional or unintentional rejection of you?

God gives us grace to go through life's toughest challenges, but also to grow through life's toughest challenges. Write about how you grew through the most difficult times in your marriage. What did you learn? What strengths did you develop? What spiritual gifts did you receive?

Initial Thoughts

Progress

Growth

More Growth

Practice of New Understanding

Mastery of New Understanding

PART IV

Parenting with Love

And these words, which I command you today, shall be on your heart. You shall teach them diligently to your children, and shall talk of them when you sit in your house, and when you walk by the way, and when you lie down, and when you rise. You shall bind them as a sign on your hand, and they shall be as frontlets between your eyes. You shall write them on the doorposts of your house and on your gates.

DEUTERONOMY 6:6–9

LET LOVE LEAD

W HEN MY OLDEST DAUGHTER, JORDAN, LEFT
home to go to college, I had to make a big adjustment, because she was going to be completely out of our
house and on her own. I remember dropping her off at college, helping unload her boxes and getting her settled into
her room. Of course, I took a little longer than necessary
because letting go is hard. As I left, I began to realize that
my baby was no longer under my immediate supervision.
She would have to make her own choices and deal with the
consequences, good or bad. All kinds of thoughts raced
through my mind, and to be honest, I was a little afraid.
I planned to call her throughout the day and planned to
check on her overnight on weekends. But I was concerned

that I would not be there to see what was really going on.

In the following weeks I frantically texted her reminders: "Remember to put God first!" "Did you get your daily bread (The Word) today?" Whenever a particular scripture came to mind, I texted her. I remember sending her a text message letting her know all the things she needed to do and not do as she embarked on this new phase of her life. She responded with a simple text that profoundly impacted me. She said, *"Mom, you are going to have to trust the foundation you've put in me."*

As I reflect on the extent to which Creflo and I tried to control every aspect of Jordan's life when she was younger, I can't help but laugh. It was hilarious at times. We were pretty adamant about our first daughter—making sure she was not swayed by negative influences. For instance, we would not allow any type of secular music programming into our house, and were always policing and trying to figure out what she was listening to or watching. We'd check her iPod and all sorts of things to make sure she was being obedient. We were afraid bad messages in certain music would compel her to bad behavior without her even realizing it. We just knew that if she was listening to *"I don't see nothing wrong with a little bump and grind,"* letting that message—or something like it—seep down into her soul could add to the pressures and temptations she would already face. We were so determined to keep out the bad music that we didn't focus enough on how we could encourage her to listen to the good music. Mainstream programming became a part of our lives. We purchased tons of Christian gospel rap CDs, but our children laughed at the quality of the music. Thankfully, the quality of gospel rap has improved, and all that struggle over music gave birth to our record label, Arrow Records, which my daughters are building with me.

In hindsight, we could have decided to operate more in faith and grace rather than in doubt and fear. We could have involved her in the decisions we made so that she wouldn't feel that we were coming down on her with an iron fist. If we had discussed our concerns about a song we forbade, for instance, she may have agreed, or helped us to appreciate a different perspective that we were overlooking. Such a discussion could have equipped her to school her peers about the messages they were training their brains on. Of course our generation had controversial music, too. Young people jammed to Patti LaBelle's "Lady Marmalade" in the seventies, and in the eighties to Marvin Gaye's "Sexual Healing" and Cyndi Lauper's "Girls Just Want to Have Fun." A discussion with our daughters, putting today's racy music in context, might have given them an appreciation for the bigger picture—about where music has been and where it may be going. We recognized their natural talent for singing and songwriting, but guiding them with faith rather than fear would have allowed us to seize more teachable moments during their formative years.

This is a primary example of what it means to parent based on the grace of God rather than on fear. We, as parents, should be willing to pause and really listen to what the Holy Spirit is saying. He is going to always lead us to the best, most loving way to teach and train our children. He is always the best guide.

When it came to dating, Creflo and I made sure we laid down the rules. We told our girls that they shouldn't even think of having a boyfriend, and their father was the only male they were going to spend quality time with. Naturally, as they became teens they were attracted to the opposite sex and wanted boyfriends!

I remember when Jordan had a crush on a boy whom we had heard some negative things about. We tried to do everything we could to prevent her from seeing him. We told her she was not to contact him in any way. It's kind of funny now, but the more we tried to keep her away from the boy, the more he would just appear! He would just literally pop up! You know why? Fear is just faith in the opposite direction, and what you continue to fear will eventually come to pass. That urge to control can be caused by a negative spirit.

We learn from our mistakes. Now that my husband and I have more revelation on grace-based parenting versus fear-based parenting, we approach situations with our children differently. Many people believe that because we are pastors our lives should be perfect. But that is simply unrealistic. We deal with the same things other parents deal with. Our children aren't perfect. However, we know that as we rely on the Holy Spirit, He will lead us in the right direction—no matter what our children do. We may wake up and discover one of our children is disobeying us or doing something we don't appreciate. In these cases, we've decided that we have to just do as we have learned and preached. We have to stay in faith, knowing that we can rely on God and His grace. We can trust Him to give us wisdom in any given situation.

Embracing Motherhood

Motherhood is something to be embraced and valued. As women, we are uniquely capable of bringing children into the world, nursing them in their formative months, and raising them until they are able to care for themselves. We are designed and conditioned to be nurturers. But we all need God's grace to successfully raise our children.

Motherhood allows us to fully express our nurturing abilities as our children grow into adulthood. When I was about to give birth to my first child, I was elated! I was looking forward to being able to shape her, nurture her, and teach her. I experienced this feeling when each of my three daughters was born. I came into motherhood with great expectations of what the future would hold for them.

When we realize that our children are gifts and assignments from God, motherhood is such a fulfilling and rewarding experience. God has given us these precious gifts to teach and train up in His ways. We must put the right values in our children, believing that when they are faced with decisions in life, they will make the right choices. The reality is that they will make the right decisions and sometimes they won't. But as mothers, we must give them a solid foundation to build upon. The Bible tells us to teach our children the Word. We took our children to Bible study, but we also discussed it at the dinner table—both at home and dining out. Sometimes we saw something while we were riding in the car or out at the mall that opened an opportunity for me to teach them what the Bible says about our interaction and behavior. Sometimes my daughters would say, "Oh, Mom, is it really that deep? Is it that serious?" when I was cautioning them about the messages they were allowing to enter their mind through music or a TV show. But whether or not they could appreciate the lessons, God said teach, so I taught whenever an opportunity presented itself. I know they will appreciate it later, as they grow up.

In addition to our three daughters, Creflo and I have had the rewarding experience of raising two wonderful sons. Creflo already had custody of Greg when we married. Greg was thirteen years old then, and he immediately started calling me mom. Not only was I a new wife, but I immediately became a new mother. A while later, we gained custody of our other adopted son, Jeremy, who works with us in the ministry. Raising them allowed me to teach, but also to be taught.

I am so grateful for the revelation we have received on grace and grace-based relationships, because it has changed the way we relate to all of our children. We allow the Holy Spirit to lead us in our relationships instead of being in bondage to rules and laws.

Born in Sin

When my oldest daughter, Jordan, was little, she found little ways to test us. When one of our assistants would try to close the car door, she'd stick her foot out so they couldn't. She kept doing it, too. Foolishness is bound in their heart. They are going to do foolish stuff.

We were all born in sin, as the Bible says. Yes, you've got little devils running around that were born in sin on this earth. Yes, they are going to want to do stuff. We allow them to make mistakes, but by being present and speaking into their life, we can help them put it all together.

Our kids are going to get into relationships with people we don't approve of. They are going to push the limits on a curfew. They may get a tattoo or body piercing we dislike. They may wear hairstyles and clothes of which we disapprove. We tell them what the Bible says. We tell them what we ourselves have learned the hard way. We set up parameters for them. We pray for them. But they have to live their lives and learn their lessons.

Just like the Prodigal Son. He could have been home living the good life, relaxing, watching a flat-screen TV with a remote in his hand. (Okay, they didn't have flat-screen TVs back then, but my point is the same: he had luxuries at home.) But the Prodigal Son left his luxuries behind. He took it for granted. He wanted to go out into the wild. He turned his back on what his father was trying to give him. Dumb stuff. As parents, we have to know that our children lack wisdom and that we are there to guide them; but some mistakes they will have to make, and some lessons, they will have to learn on their own.

Truth and Consequences

Grace is not blind. In our homes, we must establish the standard of God, and build our lifestyle based on our beliefs. We must know God's truth and speak it like Jesus spoke it. Jesus was straightforward, and He called it like it was. He called a liar a liar, a thief a thief. I like the way Iyanla Vanzant puts it: "Let's just call a thing a thing." Let's be straightforward with our children.

There are laws, and there are penalties associated with breaking those laws. We have to teach our children this. If you drive one hundred miles per hour in a sixty-five-mile-per-hour zone, you're going to get a ticket. God's grace is not a "get-out-of-jail-free" card. Grace may have afforded you the car, grace may have worked through your parents, allowing them the means and the mindset to buy you a car, but once you're in it, you must obey the rules of the road.

God is gracious and loving toward us. We may have been reckless and foolish with our lives, partying at the club, dropping it like it was hot. We may have been binge-ing out at the crack house at some point in our life. God does not hold that foolishness against us. God will be there, loving us as much as He always did. But there may be some consequences here in the world. We may end up with disease, and debt. We may end up in jail. Grace does not mean we won't have to deal with the consequences of our behavior. Teaching our children God's truth and helping them understand consequence is one of the most valuable gifts we can give them.

Let the Word of Christ dwell in
you richly in all wisdom; teaching and
admonishing one another in psalms and
hymns and spiritual songs, singing with
grace in your hearts to the Lord.

COLOSSIANS 3:16

Feed Them the Word

I was watching Joyce Meyer in a broadcast she titled "Grace for Difficult Situations." She shared the story of a woman who lost her four-year-old grandson in a car accident. The woman was driving the car that crashed, killing her grandson. She herself sustained severe injuries that would take more than a year to heal. But she was a praying woman, and she believed in the grace of God. She said that in her household they had taken Joyce Meyer's advice to heart. "One thing Joyce Meyer talks about is fighting back with the arsenal of God," the woman said. She talked about how the Word strengthened and restored her. She said she believes God is an awesome God, a God of restoration, a God of reconciliation. How could she say God restores after losing a grandchild? She had to know that although her grandson had gone home to be with the Lord, God would restore life, hope, and laughter like she had shared with her grandson. Just for sanity's sake she would repeat certain scriptures out loud. "Sometimes you have to distract yourself away from your own thoughts, so all you hear is the Word of God," she said.

I encourage you to feed your children the Word of God daily. Nourish them with God's promises in their formative years. Get it down in their bellies, so that when they are in a challenging situation—and you're nowhere around—God's Word wells up inside of them and saves the day.

The Bible tells us, "Let the Word of Christ dwell in you richly in all wisdom; teaching and admonishing one another in psalms and hymns and spiritual songs, singing with grace in your hearts to the Lord." We want to fill our children up with old hymns and new gospel music, songs of inspiration that will minister to them even when we're not around. I believe that the three-year-old child who learns to sing "This Little Light of Mine" will carry that ministering song in her heart the rest of her life. She may find herself in college, feeling overwhelmed by an assignment, or she may be in a tough situation at her job in her young adult years. That song she learned in her formative years will bubble up and minister to her. The boy who grows up singing "Jesus Loves Me" will have that ministry for the rest of his life.

They are going to have some dark days in life. They are going to have some months of despair, perhaps periods of confusion. Teach them to stay prayed up on the Word. Teach them to rely on God's grace, and stand on God's promises in their hour of need. Immerse them in the Word and teach them how to tap into God's grace so they won't become overpowered by their emotions or outside influences.

We teach more by our actions than by our words. I encourage you to demonstrate your belief in God's grace. Don't be so quick to anger. You may be frustrated in traffic or angry that someone cut you off on the highway. Instead of cursing and carrying on, your children should witness a sincere "God bless them" from you. Rather than getting into a shouting match with your spouse, your children should witness the strength of your silence, or your yielding. Because you believe God has already given you the victory, you are not quick to anger.

Listen

Many of our children are in trouble. In the United States we lose close to five thousand young people, ages ten through twenty-four, to suicide each year, according to the Centers for Disease Control. The CDC reports that violence is wreaking havoc on our youth. Beyond the newspaper headlines that alarm us when a teenager is gunned down, our young people are exposed to violence in ways we could never have imagined when we were growing up. In 2011, more than seven hundred thousand young people, ages ten through twenty-four, were treated in emergency rooms for injuries sustained from assaults. That's almost one million kids assaulted in a year. How are they coping with threats to their lives and the loss of so many of their young friends? They are coping with alcohol, drugs, and sex—anything they can get their hands on to make the pain go away. Our young people need all the love, all the prayers, all the guidance we can give them. But in order to guide them, we must listen to them. Hear them out.

Listening allows us to know where they are and what they are dealing with. Listening empowers us to pray effectively for them and guide them strategically. Sometimes my kids would yell, "You don't know what you're talking about!" I know, in some households that's enough to get a child in trouble. But I've tried to be patient and listen. Just because a child is being arrogant, doesn't mean I need to react with my own arrogance. I don't tolerate disrespect. No child of mine is going to get up in my face with their bad attitude, but if they're coming to me in a respectful manner, I will hear them out.

My mom was an educator, and she would often say, "Young people need a lot of guidance and direction. Don't say, 'Ah, you're just rebellious,' and write them off. There's a lot going on in a young person's mind. Listen to them."

It's no wonder young people have picked up on that hit song from *Dreamgirls*, "Listen." It's a heartfelt plea to be heard. Eighteen-year-old Melanie Amaro, from Sunrise, Florida, sang it with such conviction she got a standing ovation on *The X Factor*. We all want to be heard. Our children want to be heard. As parents, we must listen if we want to lead. To guide the young people in our care effectively, we must open our ears, our minds, and our hearts. Many of our young people are crying out to be heard. It's important for our children to know that they can come and speak to us about anything that's on their mind. I didn't always have that openness with my oldest daughter, but as we grew, and God guided me, our communication improved. We got to a point where we *can* have open, honest conversations.

Good parenting demands that we listen to our children, and any other young people in our care. Whether we are the parents, aunts, uncles, grandparents, or even the parent figures for our children's friends for just a few hours at a time, we need to listen. We need to pay attention to their silence, as well. Where our young folks are tuned out, we have to pay closer attention to hear what they are saying in silence. Listening to their tone, to the language of their outfits, taking note of the company they would like to keep can be opportunities to engage them in conversation and impart wisdom and guidance.

Disconnect to Reconnect

We have more distractions and temptations to contend with than our parents had when they were raising us. We've got Twitter, Facebook, Instagram, texting, sexting, and tweet, tweet, tweet. There's also Candy Crush and so many other technology-driven distractions. We must connect in ways that matter most.

I know that many parents have become as easily distracted, and prone to attention deficit disorder (ADD), as our children. But I encourage you to reduce your technology time, and request that your youngsters do the same. Maintaining good parenting while also maintaining good relationships with our children requires effective communication. Turn off the technology and talk! Some nights we've just got to turn off *Scandal*, *The Real Housewives of Atlanta*, and *Family Feud*. Some Sunday afternoons we need to turn off the NFL games, the NBA games. Discuss what's going on in your neighborhood. Get your child's opinion on an intriguing issue that's in the news. Talk to them about a certain Bible verse or some other inspiration God shined into your life that day.

Some of us had parents who limited our TV time when we were growing up. We might have gotten a total of three hours a week of TV time. They were smart enough to tell us to go outside and play with friends. They told us to run around in the park and feel the sun on our skin and the wind at our back. We can find ways to help our children better connect with us, with each other, with our community, with the very ground we walk on. If we're not inclined to follow First Lady Michelle Obama's lead and engage our children in gardening, we can at least make sure they understand that the salad they get at McDonald's was not grown in the kitchen at McDonald's. We can have discussions about where our food comes from. We can help our kids reconnect with the beauty of nature by planning more backyard picnics, and, yes, even just sitting on the ground for a change. Connect.

We have to lead by example. We want our children to learn the difference between "friends" on Facebook, and real friends—the ones who will be there for them in their times of need and in their moments of life-changing successes. If it is necessary that we show them how we express love for the friends in our lives, we're not spending excessive amounts of time posting to our "friends" in cyberspace. We want our children to understand that although the mental stimulation they can get from (and become addicted to in) video games is fun, the joy they can get from old-fashioned human interaction is so much more enriching and sustaining.

If we're constantly texting and sending notes on Facebook while we're at the dinner table or at a stoplight, we're sending the wrong signals. Let's disconnect and reconnect. We are their most important role models.

Guide Them

Luke 2:41–50 tells us that Jesus was moving into His calling at twelve years of age. He went with His parents to Jerusalem for the annual Festival of the Passover, as they had always done. But when His parents left, unbeknownst to them Jesus stayed behind at the Temple. His parents traveled home thinking their boy was with them, mixed in with the traveling crowd. When they got home, they looked for Him among their family and friends. When they could not find Him, they returned to Jerusalem. They searched everywhere for Him, growing more anxious and distraught by the moment. After three days of searching, they found Him in the Temple courts in Jerusalem, among the teachers, listening and asking questions.

"Everyone who heard him was amazed at his understanding and his answers," Luke 2:47 tells us about the boy Jesus. When His parents saw Him, they asked, "Son, why have you treated us like this? Your father and I have been anxiously searching for you." The boy-who-would-become-King said, "Why were you searching for me? Didn't you know I had to be in my Father's house?" His parents did not understand what He was saying.

Samuel, in the Bible, was just a boy when he got his calling. First Samuel 3:1–10 tells us that in the days of Samuel, messages and visions from the Lord were rare, but the boy Samuel heard a voice calling his name. At first he thought it was his teacher, Eli, calling him. But Eli was half asleep and assured the boy he had not called him. The third time Samuel went to Eli, his teacher realized the boy was being called by the Lord.

Eli told Samuel, "Go and lie down, and if He calls you again, say, 'Speak, Lord. I am your servant and I am listening.'"

Samuel went on to become a great leader of his people,

but his calling first came when he was just a boy. Thank God he had a parental guide who encouraged his calling. Eli could have told the boy he was crazy, hearing voices—"Leave me alone!" But Eli facilitated the boy's growth and helped him become what God was calling him to become.

As parents we should be the first to recognize and nurture the presence of God in our offspring. We can lead our children to become who God intended them to be. Sometimes what God calls them to be is not as obvious—to them or to us—as a gift for music or an aptitude for science and math. Sometimes we will find that our child is extraordinarily compassionate, always trying to help someone else, especially someone in distress. We may find that our child is remarkably generous, always wanting to give to others. I encourage you to help your children identify their unique talents, abilities, and inclinations, and to help them nurture those gifts in ways that can be a blessing to themselves, to their family, and to others. Help them unearth the gifts God deposited in them for their divine purpose here on earth.

I overheard a mother of a toddler talking about her baby girl's personality, which was already apparent at two.

"She's moody," the mother told her friend. "Some days when I drop her off at daycare she greets all her friends with a big hug. Sometimes she gives them the hand, she just doesn't want to be bothered. I'm explaining to two- and three-year-olds, 'She's in one of her moods today. Just leave her alone for a little while.' But I'm thinking, 'Nobody's going to put up with that moodiness when she's older. How do I allow her to have her little feelings and be in her little moods, but help her understand that behavior can have consequences?' "

Her friend, who had already raised her own children, smiled. "Unfortunately," she said, sympathizing, "parenting doesn't come with a manual. Even if it did, it would have to be modified for each child. Every one of them is different."

The Bible's guidance is most applicable here: love is patient, caring, and kind. One child may require more patience than another, but the guidance embedded in this instruction will serve you well for every child.

Pray for Guidance

Try not to get emotional about the challenges. Pray and trust God. I trust that whatever problems my young people are dealing with, God's grace will allow me to be what I need to be for them in that situation. I pray for revelation. Sometimes it comes immediately, sometimes it comes a day or a week later. I may be reminded of a particular scripture that addresses the problem, or experience a moment of clarity that guides me to the perfect scripture to address the situation. I try not to get too anxious. I pray for them, then leave them in God's hand.

There are many wonderful experiences in parenting, but sometimes parenting can be frustrating. As parents, we have to really be committed to the call of raising our children. Eventually, they'll get it, they'll understand. The Bible says, in Proverbs 22:6, "Train up a child in the way he should go: and when he is old, he will not depart from it."

I had to realize that just because I'm a Christian, that didn't mean the job of parenting would be easy. We make mistakes, and sometimes we fail as parents. But because of our beliefs, we don't give up. We stay at it.

I see Christian parents losing kids to prison all too often. I see Christian parents struggling with their children's drug and alcohol addictions, teen pregnancy, decisions to drop out of high school. I encourage parents to understand that we live in a world where there are many outside influences and distractions. We may think that because our child is with us most of the time, or because we know where they are at all times, they simply wouldn't do certain bad things. That's just not reality. The world is full of mixed messages and influences beyond our control. It's up to us as parents to help our children make sense of it all.

Young people get many confusing messages these days. This means we have to work extra hard to help them make sense of it all. For instance, the Bible tells us fornication and adultery are sins, but some of our hit TV shows and movies glamorize these behaviors. I know some adults who haven't reconciled these mixed messages for themselves; but for the sake of our children, we must be consistent in our beliefs. The Bible condemns fornication, so we don't want to condone it. We can't control the external messages they get, but we can work to help them to become aware of the messages and the impact that those messages have.

The Bible offers us grace for parenting. When we're faced with a dilemma, the Bible should be our go-to guide.

Develop Their Response Ability

Creflo and I had lots of disagreements over what's best for our children. Because I had so many material things growing up, I wanted to give our children a sense of responsibility, and teach them the importance of hard work and ethics. But because Creflo grew up without as many material things as he would have liked, he's leaned toward giving our kids everything he didn't have. He is very, very generous. When our youngest son started college, Creflo picked out a car, and he wanted to give it to him before he even finished the first semester. I suggested we use a new car as a graduation incentive. I was saying, "Let's not encourage him to think he doesn't even have to graduate from college to get a reward. Let him earn the car."

Thankfully, Jeremy did well in college. I understand that my husband wanted to bless our son with a nice car.

At the same time, I wanted to bless our son—and all of our children—with the thrill that comes from achieving a goal. I want them to experience the joy you get from working hard for something. I want them to experience that feeling of confidence you get when you reach a goal.

It was important to me that our kids understood that it wasn't that I didn't want them to have all the nice things their father wanted to give them; I just wanted them to know how things work in the real world. In the real world, nobody's going to just give you a paycheck. Nobody's going to just give you a car because they love you. In the real world you have to work hard, set goals, and contribute something in order to make a living. In the real world you have to show up on time. You have to be dependable. You have to complete tasks.

Our two eldest daughters work for me, and Jeremy, our youngest son works with Creflo. We've made it clear to them: Just because you work for your parents doesn't mean you can slack off. You're expected to work hard. We are accountable for teaching them responsibility. But we also want to teach them grace, which God gives us unwarranted. There's no formula for how much grace you should give a child; similar to what God does for us. I encourage parents to pray for revelation about what to give and how much. You have to ask yourself, "Can they handle this privilege? Will it be good for them?" Whether you're considering buying a cell phone or a car, ponder the impact. Can this child handle this? You learn as you go.

As parents we have to teach our children how to clean their rooms, and clean their home. We have to teach them how to live together peaceably as a family. We have to teach them the importance of giving of themselves, of giving back. We have to teach them, for instance, the importance of spending time with their grandparents, or spending time with people who may be sick, because of how it can help the other person feel better.

All this teaching we do can pay off in dividends of joy. It's a joy for me to see my daughters grow in their music ministry. They work with me in building a record label. Hopefully someday they will run the label. I love seeing Jeremy work with his father, learning the business side of operating a church. Parenting is hard work, and it involves lots of sacrifice, but it returns to you a tremendous joy— especially in witnessing them performing their purpose and passion. It's a joy to see your child grow into their God-given purpose.

Grow with Them

You have to continue to be there for them and advise them. I know it's difficult to keep pouring guidance into someone who doesn't want to listen, someone who has their mind made up. It may feel like they're rejecting your hard-won wisdom when they are rejecting your offerings. But that's when you pray and ask God to allow you to be what He needs you to be in their life.

Understand that your role will evolve as they mature. When they were babies and made a mess, you were there to clean it up. As young adults, there will be some messes you will have to watch them clean up on their own. Your role at that point may be one of cheerleader, reminding them that they have the strength and wherewithal to clean up a mess they made by being disobedient, or exercising poor judgment.

We've got to be able to put the promises of God in their heart and let them go. That puts us in a place of vulnerability, of transparency, at risk of being hurt, at risk of being taken advantage of, but that's how God demonstrates His love to us. God is willing to let us go and make mistakes, and still be available as our Redeemer. The redemptive type of love is a love that goes all out for the sake of another. That's what we have to be willing to offer our children. And when they get to a certain age, we have to know how to deal with them as adult children. We've got to grow as they grow. We have to expect that our role in their lives will change over time. We can continually ask the Holy Spirit to guide us as to what role to play in their lives so that they can mature and develop and become rational adults. We want them to be able to make their own decisions. We want them to become independent and confident enough to hear the Holy Spirit for themselves. That's what God is after. I believe that's the fullness of the plan of God.

As parents, we hate to see our children going down the wrong path. We shake our heads and wonder, "Why are you doing that?" We try to redirect them. Sometimes they listen, sometimes they have to get out there and learn from their own mistakes. But sometimes mistakes are the best teacher.

As parents, we have to allow them to go and grow. And often we find we're doing better with the younger ones than we did with the older ones, right?

Remember the Prodigal Son. His father had to let him go out into the world and do his own thing—drinking wine and womanizing. But when the son returned home, his father was right there with an open heart. We can grow in our patience as we watch our children grow, praying for them to "come home" to the good sense God gave them. We can grow in our faith as we watch God work wonders in their life, opening doors of opportunity for them and prospering their lives. We can grow in gratitude, thanking God for their milestone moments: a hard-won "A" on an exam; becoming valedictorian at school; getting into the college of their choice; getting married; giving birth to children of their own.

Don't Give Up

I heard about a woman named Isabel who had been raised in a Southern Baptist church in a small dusty town in North Carolina. Her father was a pastor, and every week he drove his nine children to church. She loved it. When she grew up, she kept her faith and the religious traditions she was raised in. She married a Christian man in a Christian church. They had two children, and together they took their two children to church every Sunday, just as she had been raised to do.

When Isabel was sixty-seven years old, her beloved husband of forty-two years died of cancer. She was devastated. The life that she had built seemed to be unraveling. She felt disoriented. Her children had moved to other states to work in their chosen professions and raise their own children. Isabel packed her belongings and relocated to the state where her son lived with his wife and children, hoping to reconnect with him and her grandchildren. But that didn't work out too well, because the younger folks never had time to spend with her, except on holidays.

About a year after Isabel's husband died, she was diagnosed with breast cancer. A month after she was diagnosed, her daughter, who had just turned forty, was also diagnosed. Isabel continued to pray for herself and her daughter, but a year later her daughter died.

Needing to get her bearings, Isabel returned to the town where she grew up. She joined a church similar to the one her father had pastored many years before. Little by little, she regained her strength. Little by little, she got her sense of joy back. She registered at a senior center, where she enjoyed taking trips to the theater to see plays, trips to the movies, and the company of others in their golden years. A few days after Isabel celebrated her seventy-ninth birthday with friends at the senior center, she got a call that her son, her eldest child—her only surviving child—was in the hospital. Immediately she booked a flight to visit him in the intensive care unit at the hospital in the town where he lived.

When she arrived, she could not hold back the tears. Her son, a once bulky, muscular Marine, appeared withered and extremely weak. He lay flat on his back in a hospital bed with tubes and wires connected to his arms and chest. When the doctor delivered the diagnosis, it hit Isabel hard: cirrhosis of the liver. Her son's drinking problem had been worse than she knew. The doctors told her that unless he received a liver transplant he would die within six months. But in order to receive a transplant, her son would have to agree to enroll in an alcoholism rehabilitation program. Her son, fifty-four years old, married, with a young daughter, refused to submit to rehabilitation. Less than six months later he died.

Isabel was again devastated, but she never lost her faith.

Every Sunday, even when she was visiting her sisters in another state, she insisted on going to church. When asked how she could love God after losing so much, she simply said, "God's ways are not our ways. God has a reason for everything He does. I don't pretend to understand Him, but I trust Him. God has never let me down."

She knew her son's soul belonged to God before she gave birth to him here on earth, and she knew his soul returned to God. It's easy to become bitter and lose faith when it seems like everything you worked and sacrificed for gets lost—or taken away. When a child gets in trouble with the law, it seems as if all your sacrifices to get them to Sunday school every week have been for naught. When a child dies, whether from natural causes, as a result of bad choices, or from an act of violence, it is an enormous test of our faith. We feel as if we're left with nothing but ashes after a life lived on fervent, fiery prayer. Yet when times are toughest, we must stand strong on the faith we've gained over the years.

Losing a child is hard for any parent, regardless of their offspring's age. We simply do not expect to bury our children. But God's love and grace can comfort us even through such a loss. How can we experience God's love even at a time of loss? The Bible tells us, in Revelation 21:4, "And He shall wipe away every tear from their eyes; and there shall no longer be any death; there shall no longer be any mourning, or crying, or pain." That is a reminder that the grief we feel will not last always. The aching will subside. We don't want to ignore the sadness, or deny the anguish. But knowing God loves us and gives us grace in all areas of our lives, we can rest assured that the sadness will pass. We know that God's love will rise again in our life as surely as tomorrow's morning sun.

Trusting God's love in our lives, we find ways to honor the child we love. We may establish a scholarship in their memory, or donate to a charity in their honor. We find ways to keep their love alive. We thank God for the time we had with them. We trust that God had a loving reason for calling them home. We consider that God gave them their angel wings early.

I see the devastation of parents who did all they could to train up their children in the way they should go. They attended PTA meetings and devoted evenings and weekends to driving their children to dance lessons, team sports, and club meetings. They paid good money for karate classes, horseback riding lessons, choir robes, and other activities they believed would enhance their child's development. But somehow, despite all these good intentions, the child strayed from the path.

I talk to parents all the time who are struggling with a child who has gotten off track. I've met parents whose children were wayward for twenty or thirty years—on and off drugs, in and out of jail, failing at jobs—before they came to their senses.

I remind them that the Bible tells us, in 1 Corinthians 13:7, "Love never gives up, never loses faith, is always hopeful, and endures through every circumstance." When a child is spinning out of control, addicted to alcohol or drugs, caught up in a gang, running with a bad crowd, in and out of court, in and out of jail, a praying parent has to know that God is in control. We have to constantly remind our children who they are—and *whose* they are.

*For Jehovah God is our light
and protector. He gives us grace and
glory. No good thing will He withhold
from those who walk His paths.*

PSALMS 84:11

Appreciating My Own Mother

I think about my relationship with my mother sometimes. As a young teenager, I thought my mother didn't understand what I was going through. When I became a mother to teenagers, I realized she understood more than I could have imagined at that age. My mother was a high school counselor, and very much in touch with the needs of young people. I understand her intentions now, although I didn't understand her parenting back then. Her objective was the same as that of most mothers: she wanted me to succeed in life.

When my mother went home to be with the Lord, the separation anxiety I experienced was tremendous. It all happened so quickly. Like the blowing of the wind, she was gone. Of course, I was saddened by her departure. It hurt. I complained bitterly—*"God, why didn't you give her at least seventy years, like you promised every Believer?"* But the Lord answered me, saying, *"Be thankful that she lived as long as she did."* It totally changed my perspective, from complaining about the years she didn't get to celebrating the years that she did live. I began to saturate myself in the Word every chance I got. I began meditating on the fact that my mother had been a significant part of my past, and as I believed she went to heaven, I felt that she would also be a part of my future.

Losing a parent is often a life-changing experience.

Sometimes people become so buried in their grief at the loss that they never get beyond the experience. They hold on to it for years. Some turn their backs on God, the Church, and the people who love them because they are angry or afraid. I didn't want to do that. I had to take control of my emotions to prevent these emotions from ruining the rest of my life. I began to better appreciate the value my mother brought to my life. My mother was a jewel of a woman: smart, honest, savvy, and independent in ways that impressed and encouraged me. My mother was keen on education, determined that my brothers and I would all go to college. My mother's nurturing went beyond our home and extended to caring about other children, too—students she taught, and children in our neighborhood.

My mother was a strong, tenacious woman. She was loving and caring. She was also a terrific cook. People would gather around to eat her good food and hear her humorous stories. Although I greatly miss her, I've decided to celebrate her life rather than mourn over her passing. I've decided to learn from all that she has imparted to me. As a result, I started the Ethel Bolton Scholarship Fund in her memory. This fund provides scholarships for deserving students who want to go to college but need financial aid.

Practical Application

As mothers, we have all made many mistakes, and will continue to make them. However, we cannot beat ourselves up about them. Satan dwells in an atmosphere of condemnation and shame. But God wants us to know that, although we are not perfect, we can boldly come before His throne of grace to ask for help when we need it. Our responsibility is to believe and receive His love and grace so that we can effectively distribute that love and grace to others.

*And he shall be like a tree firmly
planted and tended by the streams of
water, ready to bring forth its fruit in
its season; its leaf also shall not fade or
wither; and everything he does shall
prosper and come to maturity.*

PSALMS 1:3

Get Rooted—Branch Out

I like the inspiration we get from American speed skater Emily Scott, who overcame tremendous odds just to make it to the 2014 Winter Olympic Games in Sochi. Here was a child being raised by a single father because her mother was in and out of jail for trafficking drugs. According to one NBC news report, Emily began skating at the age of six, when she tagged along with her big sister to the local skating rink.

When Emily was in third grade, however, her mother went to jail and Emily went to live with her father. He soon noticed she was very fast on skates and began to encourage her to compete. He would drive her to competitions near their home, and as she grew more competitive, he drove her to state and regional competitions. By the time she was ready for high school, she moved to Florida to train year round. At sixteen she won a gold medal as an amateur or rookie in the World Speed Championships hosted in China. She tried out for the 2010 Winter Olympics but didn't make the team. She wasn't discouraged, though. She placed tenth and believed she could make the team next time.

Her father worked hard but struggled to make ends meet. Emily secured sponsors, but about a year before the 2014 Olympics would begin, her sponsorship funds were cut from about $2,000 a month to $600 because of the problems her sponsors, U.S. Speedskating, faced. She was working at a factory in Salt Lake City, where she lived and trained, but her job didn't pay enough for her to maintain her expenses. She panicked. But friends and people she met encouraged her to engage in a little online fundraising. In the first two months, hardly anyone responded to her call for cash. Then *USA Today* got wind of her story and published an article about her fundraising efforts. With that publicity, she surpassed her initial goal of raising $15,000 to make it to the 2014 Games. She raised close to $50,000 as donations continued to pour in.

Emily competed in the Olympic Short Track races and began placing in the top five early on. On the day before her twenty-fifth birthday, she won a race and pressed on, hoping for a medal. Her commitment to follow her Olympic dream—along with her determination to train and prepare for the big event, and her faith that strangers she met on the Internet might come through with funding—prevailed.

She did not call it grace, and she didn't publicly thank God in the interviews I saw. But I know God's grace when I see it. God's grace shows up as unexpected provisions. Here it showed up as encouragement from people Emily never met in person, people willing to send five, ten, even a thousand dollars to help her get to the Olympics.

The Word informs us, in Psalms 1:3, "And he shall be like a tree firmly planted and tended by the streams of water, ready to bring forth its fruit in its season; its leaf also shall not fade or wither; and everything he does shall prosper and come to maturity."

Emily and her father were firmly planted in the desire God gave Emily to compete in the Olympics. Streams of resources flowed to them through jobs they secured, sponsorships they received, and donations raised online. Sometimes they worried about whether her dream of competing in the Olympics would come true. They had moments of doubt and despair, but they continued to work toward their goal and believed it could happen.

I encourage you to get firmly planted in the dreams and visions God has shown you for yourself and your family. Believe that God will send you the resources you need to bring your dream to fruition. Meditate on God's word when you're inclined to worry. God tells us we are already blessed, as blessed as a tree planted by a stream of water. God is our stream, our constant nourishment. God says we are already blessed.

God promises us that, like a tree, we will bring forth fruit in due season. You don't have to go begging and pleading to God ("Lord if I can get my child to act right I will feel blessed . . ."). God has already promised that our family is blessed. Thank God for blessing your child and trust that you will see the fruits of God's work in your child, and through your child, in due season. You don't have to cry for a husband. Thank God for your husband right now and delight in how God will reveal His plan for bringing a husband into your life. If God put in your heart a strong desire for a husband, rest assured that God already has a plan on how and when best to satisfy that desire He put in your heart.

Embrace Love

In our families, we experience our first lessons in love—and loss. We experience God's love most intensely in our family, because our family relationships are often our closest relationships, and also are our oldest relationships, spanning our entire lifetime. In healthy family relationships, we learn to trust. We learn to rely on someone other than ourselves. Our capacity for love—giving and receiving it—expands.

Family is the nucleus unit of any society. Although modern science allows us to create life in a petri dish, I believe God designed humans—like all other animals—to be born of a male and a female union in the context of family according to His divine plan for our spiritual development. Family grounds us and grows us. We first learn how to relate to others through our family relationships. We learn to change and adapt according to the needs of our family. For instance, a mother will notice the subtle moves and shiftings of her baby in her womb. As the baby squirms and moves about, the mother will adjust her body to make the baby more comfortable. Sometimes I think back to the days when I carried my own babies. Tending to their tiniest needs, I began to understand that God tends to our smallest needs just as well.

The late Dr. Dorothy I. Height, former president of the National Council of Negro Women, understood the importance of family. She and the NCNW led an annual Black Family Reunion on the National Mall in Washington, D.C., for more than twenty-five years to celebrate the importance of family. Her events drew more than 250,000 people from across the country to celebrate family. She knew the importance of family, and she was dedicated to restoring black families, which suffered disintegration through generations of slavery and withering discrimination.

Nourish Others

I come from a family of great cooks. My mother and grandmother were two of the best. My grandmother's good home cooking would include her signature fried chicken, biscuits, and cakes! She made it all from scratch. My grandmother used to say, "Whenever you cook, cook with love."

My mother was such a good cook that friends and family were always hinting that they were "always free, anytime, to come over," just to get some of her good soul food. In her later years, she would jokingly say, "I don't even want John to come over here anymore because he always wants me to cook!" But my mother truly enjoyed cooking. She enjoyed people and loving them through her jokes and good food. It came from a place of love, and we all knew it.

When we experience love, we know it deep inside. There's an old saying: "Good love feeds you like grub; bad love drains you like a tub." When we are experiencing and expressing God's love in our family relationships, we get filled up with laughter. We share fond memories and create wonderful new experiences. Some families get together for birthdays and holidays and any other occasions they can use as an excuse to gather at someone's home.

Forgive

I heard about a young woman named Laila, who was raised in church and learned to love Jesus. "I was going to church even before I was born, while in my mother's womb," she said laughing. At a young age, Laila asked her mother what she could do to get into heaven. Her mother said all she needed to do was give her heart to the Lord by proclaiming her belief in Him and praying to Him. Laila recited the Salvation Prayer daily, just as her mother told her. Some days those beliefs comforted her when she looked at her brother with envy because he seemed to be her parents' favorite. "I didn't have the same connection with them. He was the center of their attention, and I often felt ostracized," Laila said. Some days her silent prayers could not soothe her aching heart.

Laila craved affection. She found it with her high school sweetheart. Around this same time, Laila's parents embraced a new religion and began going to a different church than the one where Laila grew up. Laila said her parents' new church had more rules and requirements than what she had been used to. There were rules against wearing makeup and jewelry, she said. Laila was fifteen and the transition was proving to be too much for her. She was expected to fast every week. Her father became a deacon in the church and her mother became a deaconess. Laila wanted to please them, and she was very respectful. But all her good manners and well-intended fasting and praying did not stop her longings for affection. Her prayers did not settle the religious confusion swirling in her mind.

Laila grew closer to her boyfriend and they became intimate despite her knowledge that fornication was a sin. When Laila got pregnant, she and her boyfriend decided that getting an abortion seemed like the best option. She said they were so young, naïve, and bewildered, they ended up in a pro-life clinic when they thought they had been led to an abortion clinic. Laila said after sitting through a video of a baby being aborted, she felt traumatized and changed her mind about getting an abortion. She decided to go home and reconsider her options.

Laila became sicker as the days went by. She vomited to

the extent that she became severely dehydrated. Her mother had to rush her to a hospital. Once the doctors ran tests on Laila, they found out she was pregnant. She felt her mother's disappointment, and she felt badly about letting her parents down. She felt so ashamed, she could barely look at her father and avoided him as much as she could. She felt condemned at church. An elder in the church told her that in order for her to be right with God again she would have to confess her sin in front of the congregation, and apologize for it. Laila wanted to be right with God again, so she did as she was told.

Laila wanted to be right with the people in her parents' church, so she humbled herself as she was asked to do. She said while she was confessing, she felt something like the presence of God come over her, assuring her that she was forgiven. She said she felt like Jesus getting baptized. But in the next few days her feelings of guilt and shame returned. She became sick again, vomiting violently. She could not keep any food in her stomach. Her weight dropped from one hundred forty pounds to ninety-one pounds by the time she was five months pregnant. She had to return to the hospital emergency room, but this time she had to be admitted. She had to be fed through an IV, and the doctors determined she needed psychological help. They suggested that she was subconsciously trying to "vomit up the baby."

Laila's mother didn't think she needed psychological help. Instead, she brought in ministers from her church to pray for Laila. Laila's health improved a little and she was discharged from the hospital. At home she fell into a deep depression again, and soon the involuntary vomiting returned. Her mother asked the pastor of their church to pray for her. Laila remembered the prayer because of its profound effect on her. She said the pastor became strangely repetitious and loud as if he were speaking to and challenging a demonic force in their midst. She said the pastor shouted, "God loves you! God loves you! God loves you! God loves you!" and while he shouted those words over her, she felt like a physical stronghold inside of her was breaking.

After that intervention prayer, she began to tell herself that God loves her. Her heart began to heal. She felt less depressed. She decided against returning to the church where she had felt condemned by the people even though the pastor had come through for her. She decided to stay home on Sunday mornings and develop her personal relationship with God. Her daughter was born three months premature, weighing one pound and nine ounces. Her tiny lungs were underdeveloped, and she would need the support of a small oxygen tank for months. Laila named her baby girl and began bonding with her, but doctors tried to prepare her for the worst. They told Laila that if her baby lived, she could expect her to have health problems for the rest of her life. But God's love prevailed.

At forty-three years of age, Laila began sharing her testimony at the new church she joined. She and her healthy daughter, Shawn, who was now a lovely and beautiful twenty-four-year-old, hoped their testimony could encourage others. Laila said her daughter had proved the doctors wrong. They had said Shawn would have learning disabilities growing up, but Shawn excelled in school, ranking in the top ten percent of her high school graduating class. Shawn even went on to pursue her master's degree.

One day, Shawn asked her mother why she was named Shawn, and her mother explained that she had felt that was the name God wanted her to have. When she was pregnant, Laila said, God put it on her heart to name her baby Shawn. Now that Shawn was grown-up and asking questions about her identity, her mother decided to look up the meaning of the name. Laila was pleasantly surprised to find that she had unknowingly named her baby with the Hebrew word that means "God is gracious."

Laila said it took her a while to forgive her parents and their church, but after years of prayer and soul-searching, she was able to forgive them all. She even has a loving relationship with her parents today. Years after the incident of her forced confession at the altar of her parents' church, she saw one of the ministers who had pressured her into confessing. She was delighted that their chance encounter had not stirred any feelings of resentment or bitterness in her. Her intentions to forgive him had been complete. She said she was able to embrace him sincerely and wish him well.

Laila was able to demonstrate God's love and grace through her forgiveness.

Let Love Reign

Choosing to walk in love is not always easy. Regardless of the situation and circumstances we face, God enables us to forgive. He wants us to show love through the act of forgiveness. Walking in love by choosing to forgive is not based on how we feel; it is a decision we make *by faith*. We walk by faith, not by sight. As we walk by faith, we choose to do the opposite of what *feels* right. We deny selfish motives and refuse to satisfy our hurt feelings. I believe that when we make the quality decision to love and forgive by faith, God empowers us, and our feelings eventually line up with our decision.

In 1 Corinthians 13:8 the Bible says love never fails. This means that no matter what was done to us, if we choose love's route, the outcome will *always* work out in our favor. If we can trust nothing else, still, we can know without a shadow of a doubt that handling the situation God's way will always succeed, even though it may not look like success in society's eyes.

I met a woman who said she felt intimidated when she was called into a meeting with the director of the agency where she worked and his personnel director. She knew they were calling her to account for her supervisor's complaints about her productivity. She felt that she had been unfairly criticized and was being unfairly called to account. She prayed in the minutes leading up to the meeting. She sat quietly at her desk with her head bowed in prayer. She marched into the meeting with more confidence than she had before praying. When the meeting began, she said later, she felt as if the Holy Spirit had come through her, speaking with a boldness she had never been known to have. She asserted herself. She told them how she was a hard worker, and about classes she had taken to improve her value to the agency. A few months later, she was called back into a meeting with the personnel director and offered a promotion. Rather than get angry at her supervisor and level counteraccusations to make her supervisor look bad, she prayed and allowed God to guide her.

Even when God doesn't immediately deliver us from a bad boss or unpleasant coworker, we can choose to act in love rather than fear in that relationship. We should approach each day as if it is a new day. Go into the office thinking about how God can speak a word of kindness or encouragement that day. Thinking about what someone said the day before that upset you, or what they said the day before that, is like carrying around dead weight, and it will only make the situation between the two of you worse. Let go of the weights of the past. Lighten up. Think about what you can say to that person today to make your relationship better. Pray for the right words at the right time. Pray each day, expecting that it might be the day God changes the situation between the two of you.

In the world, when it comes to forgiving others, there are conditions attached to it. Forgiveness, according to the world's standards, is based on feelings, circumstances, and whether the other person is willing to change. If we try to forgive based on our feelings or the other person's actions, forgiveness may never happen. Sometimes those who hurt or offend us do not realize that they have wronged us. Or they may simply refuse to see things from our point of view. Forgiving someone does not mean we condone their past behavior. It does not mean we have to accept their bad behavior or allow them to hurt us again. It means we recognize that something they said or did is different from what we consider acceptable.

Forgiving others simply means to pardon them of an offense. The Bible tells us, in Matthew 5:44, "Love your enemies, bless those who curse you, do good to those who hate you, and pray for those who spitefully use you and persecute you."

This is not an instruction to be passive. This is a call for us to shine God's light into the darkest situations. We see it, for instance, when a nurse is working with a belligerent patient. The patient, who may be in more pain than he can articulate, may be cursing and yelling at the nurse. But what does the nurse do? She doesn't turn her back on him and walk away; she gives him medicine to ease his pain. In our lives, we, too, can administer the medicine of God's love in response to others' offenses.

When someone cuts us off in traffic, instead of trailing them, honking our horns in road rage, we can send them a prayer, asking God to slow them down before they hurt themselves or someone else. When we feel slighted at work, instead of scheming on how to retaliate, we can ask that God bless the coworker or boss so they don't have to behave badly.

When we are full of God's grace, we don't get irritated when we're in line at the grocery store and someone has not only entered the ten-items-or-less express lane with a cart full of stuff, but they are insisting on paying with a check, slowing the process down even further. Instead of rolling our eyes at them or calling for a manager to come and kick them out of the express lane, we offer a smile and a prayer: "God bless you. You must be in a bigger hurry than me!"

Unforgiveness is a negative emotion that can have a serious effect on our souls and even our physical health. It is like dirt clogging up the pipeline to our relationship with God, blocking the channels that enable His power to flow into our lives. We think we are hurting those who hurt us, but we are actually hurting ourselves. It is like we are keeping ourselves chained to those who hurt us, while they go on with their lives. It's just not worth it.

When we don't forgive, we also allow bitterness into our hearts and minds. Bitterness is like a poisonous root that infects us with negativity. The Bible says bitterness defiles us when we allow it to spring up in our lives. Forgiveness is the answer that liberates us from every negative emotion connected to an offense.

In her *New York Times* best-seller *Anatomy of the Spirit*, Dr. Caroline Myss writes that even physical healing is possible through forgiving. She writes, "Forgiveness is a spiritual act of perfection, but it is also a physically healing act. Forgiveness is no longer merely an option, but a necessity for healing." She notes that Jesus first healed his patients' emotional suffering in order to remedy their physical ailments. She shares numerous stories of individuals whose physical sickness—from minor aches and pains to life-threatening cancers—could be rooted in unforgiveness.

Refusing to forgive causes everything in our body to slow down—digestion, circulation, all our bodily functions. Anger and bitterness form a shield around us, blocking love from getting in.

I believe another reason why forgiveness is so vital in the life of a Christian is because it demonstrates the grace of God to others, and allows others to see that our relationship with Him is real. As Christians, we send a message to others by the way we live. As we spend time in God's Word and in His presence, we are strengthened and empowered to handle situations that challenge our love walk. Additionally, spending time in His presence and in His Word matures us and allows us to see situations through His eyes. In today's society, the attitude of forgiveness is not easily seen. We live in a time when the prevailing attitude stresses "do what feels right," and "an eye for an eye." Having a forgiving attitude that is quick to overlook an offense is not the norm. This is why it speaks so loudly when we choose to respond to an offense with love instead of anger. People can sense something different about us when we do so. They begin to see the very nature of God operating through us. As we continue to make decisions to forgive, regardless of who offends us, we continue to position ourselves to receive and demonstrate God's empowerment of grace.

Grace doesn't erase consequences, however. The Bible tells us, in Proverbs 19:19, "A man of great wrath will suffer punishment . . . for if you rescue him, he will do it again." God is not calling for us to be doormats and allow people to walk all over us, like the belligerent hospital patient who is physical with those who try to help him. But we can pray for them.

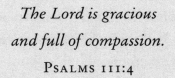

*The Lord is gracious
and full of compassion.*

PSALMS 111:4

Ride Out Your Storms

Every family faces storms. Storms are misunderstandings and disagreements—storms of lack, or floods of abundance. Obstacles will come. Hard times will come. That is the law of nature, the law of this physical world we live in. We have to recognize whether our family's foundation is built on the solid ground of faith or on the shifting sands of circumstance. We must be grounded in the Word of God, so that when the strong winds of change blow we do not get tossed about. We can stand on the Word of God.

The Bible tells us, "The rain came down, the streams rose, and the winds blew and beat against that house; yet it did not fall because it had its foundation on the rock" (Matthew 7:25).

When storms come, we can be grounded in God's rock-solid love and grace. When we have rooted ourselves in what the Bible tells us about God's love and grace, we know that no weapon formed against us will prosper. When our child—or any young person in our family—is facing a bully, we stand with them, assuring them that their enemies cannot defeat them. When a loved one is in a storm of malicious gossip or a public controversy, we can help them stand strong on God's promise that they will be victorious.

When we have invested time to root ourselves in what God promises, we are prepared when our loved ones face a storm of grief brought on by a tragic loss. We are prepared to anchor our loved ones when they face a storm of despair bought on by unexpected unemployment. We are prepared to gird a loved one through his or her storm of divorce.

When you're rooted in God's love, and believing in God's grace, you can provide relief in the midst of a storm. You can explain to your loved ones that their storm doesn't necessarily mean God is punishing them. You can assure them that God is not mad at them. You can convince them that God loves them. You can be encouraging and supportive.

In the midst of a storm you can remind your loved ones that storms come to test our strengths and compel us to build new spiritual muscles. You can encourage your loved ones to pull closer to God during difficult times rather than withdraw from God and the people God put in their life to help them. The Bible says we should bear one another's burdens. Galatians 6:2 tells us, "Bear ye one another's burdens, and therefore fulfill the law of Christ." God grounds us in His love and grace in order for us to extend His love and grace to our loved ones in their time of need. The love and grace God gives to us is not solely for us.

Sometimes storms come because of disobedience. That was the case with Jonah. Jonah fell on hard times because he disobeyed God. He went in the opposite direction God was telling him to go. While he was out there doing his own thing, following his own plan, his own agenda, all kinds of things started happening to him. He was swallowed up by a whale because he was disobedient to God. But God, in His everlasting love, delivered Jonah from the belly of the beast, and set Jonah on solid ground again.

We can experience storms as punitive or empowering. When we become focused on God's love and grace, we will come out of a storm—and help our loved ones come out of their storms—better, stronger, and wiser than we were prior to the storm.

A storm of employment anxiety—frustration with management, feeling stuck in a rut—may seem to you like a punishment of some kind. It may feel like you're being punished for neglecting to complete a college degree, or punished for declining a particular project in a previous year. But knowing that God loves you and promises you victory, you become empowered. You apply for other jobs within your company and elsewhere. You enroll in professional development courses. You pray for divine revelation about where to look and how best to proceed in improving your employment satisfaction. You expect God's grace, that unmerited favor, to materialize. You come out of that storm of anxiety assured that God has a plan for you. You come out of it with more faith than you had going in.

Jesus was gracious and full of compassion. Storms provide us opportunities to demonstrate grace and compassion to our loved ones. Storms are opportunities for us to experience God's miraculous favor in our lives. God uses storms to reveal our faith. When we are faithful that God loves us, we embrace the authority He has given us through the knowledge of Jesus Christ. We begin to use that authority the way Jesus did. The Bible tells us, "Then He arose and rebuked the wind, and said to the sea, 'Peace be still,' And the wind ceased and there was great calm" (Mark 4:39). If Jesus had not trusted God, knowing God loved Him and would bring Him through the storm, He might have died out at sea. Knowing that God loves us, we can be the rock in our family. Our families do not have to be set adrift or torn asunder by winds of change, by illnesses, by tragedies, by confusion all around. Being grounded in God's love, believing in God's grace, we can be peace for our family in the midst of a storm.

I encourage you to experience God's love in every situation. Ask yourself, "How does God get the glory out of this?" When we understand that God loves us, we look for His love in every situation. It may feel like a punishment that the man you married left you with three children to raise on your own. But instead of feeling bad, beating yourself up, thinking you should have listened to the people who told you not to marry him, embrace and bask in the knowledge that God loves you even when you make mistakes.

Journal Questions

OPENING PRAYER

Father God, I come to You with expectation that You will manifest more of Your love and grace in my family. God, I thank You for pouring Your good thoughts into me through Your Holy Word. God, I thank You for increasing my appreciation of my family, I thank You for reminding me of how You have already blessed my family, and for giving me a divine vision of Your purpose for my family. God, I pray for Your divine protection over my family, and pray that Your love and grace flow to each individual and to us as a group.

1. Do you feel condemned and/or ashamed about past mistakes you've made as a mother?

2. Have you prayed and received God's forgiveness? Have you forgiven yourself for your past mistakes?

3. What would God's grace and love feel like to you? What does it look like to you?

4. How can you exemplify God's love and grace to your children?

5. How can you help your children develop a personal relationship with God?

6. How can you show your children your love for God and your belief in God's grace?

7. Count it all as joy: make a list of the five most challenging situations you experienced with your family or because of your family.

8. Consider the lessons, or spiritual gifts, God may have been offering you through those experiences.

9. Choose one from those five experiences and write God a thank-you note for the experience.

Initial Thoughts

Breakthrough

Growth

More Growth

Practice of New Understanding

Mastery of New Understanding

ACKNOWLEDGMENTS

First and foremost, I would like to thank God, my family on earth and in heaven (my mom and grandparents). Tracy and Sonsyrea, you were sent by God to help me complete this project. I'd like to especially thank Tawanda Mills and our publications department, along with Gurie, for their dedicated commitment from the beginning to the very end. Also, I am thankful for Carol Mann, and all of the fearless, radical women at World Changers and in Prestige Ministry who have inspired me to leap to new heights. My prayer is that this book will inspire each of you to fully experience all the love that God has for you.

With all my heart,

PT

Taffi Dollar is a world-renowned author, teacher, and conference speaker. Together with her husband, Creflo Dollar, she pastors World Changers Church International (WCCI) and World Changers Church-New York. She founded the WCCI Women's Ministry as well as Prestige Ministry, both geared toward assisting and empowering women. She serves as the CEO of Arrow Records, a Christian recording company, and as a guest panelist for numerous music festivals and workshops. Taffi holds a bachelor's degree in Mental Health and Human Services. She lives in Atlanta with her husband and five children.